The Best Contemporary Women's Humor

EDITED BY ROZ WARREN

Introduction by Nancy A. Walker, Ph.D.

The Crossing Press, Freedom, CA 95019

Cover cartoon by Nicole Hollander
Cover design by Nicole Hollander and Tom Greensfelder
Book design by Amy Sibiga
Printed in the U.S.A.

Library of Congress Cataloging-in-Publication Data
The best contemporary women's humor / edited by Roz Warren.
p. cm.
ISBN 0-89594-694-7 (pbk.)
1. Women--Humor. I. Warren, Rosalind, 1954- .
PN6231.W6B39 1994
808.88'2--dc20
94-13173
CIP

CONTENTS

THIS BOOK IS DEDICATED WITH LOTS OF LOVE TO ANN COLLETTE AND ALIVIA CROOKS

INTRODUCTION

It certainly would have made things easier for me if Roz Warren had begun editing her Women's Humor books fifteen years ago. That's when I started to do research on women's humor—when it wasn't clear yet that a woman could be a feminist and have a sense of humor. In fact, it wasn't clear that a *woman* could have a sense of humor, unless that meant laughing at jokes that frequently demeaned women. (And as I write this, in the fall of 1993, the United States Supreme Court is hearing arguments in the case of a woman who claims that her male employer's crude sexual joking constituted sexual harassment. He probably thinks she has no sense of humor.) By now, with Roz's third women's humor anthology, anyone who is paying attention knows how creatively and variously women use humor to steady themselves in a chaotic world that still denies them many forms of equality. Reading this volume is like participating in a conversation with a group of smart, witty people who know how absurd life can be, and who restore their—and our—balance *by* pointing it out.

The Best Contemporary Women's Humor illustrates what is both traditional and new about women's humorous expression. The fact that reading it reminds me of a conversation echoes the historical reality that women have typically felt free to express themselves humorously in women-only groups rather than in mixed-sex gatherings, not only because men have tended to take the floor in such gatherings, but also because one of the things women have poked fun at is their relationships with men—sitting around kitchen tables, giggling in the dark, writing in the pages of women's magazines. The requisite seven and a half hours of talk that Stephanie Brush writes about in "In Praise of Best Girlfriends" probably includes at least three hours of laughter.

Because of its more or less underground existence, women's humor has employed subversive strategies when it has emerged aboveground, masking its message beneath the happy-but-harried housewives of Phyllis McGinley and Shirley Jackson, or emerging slyly from Dorothy Parker's laments about faithless lovers. But yesterday's subversion is today's confrontation, it seems. Anxiety about homemaking effectiveness may still be an issue for some women, but Liz Scott manages to one-up her compulsively neat neighbor in "How to Out-Tidy a Tideybole," and Wendy Cope achieves the grace of Dorothy Parker in "I Worry," with its dagger-thrust of a last line.

Traditionally, too, women's humor has been preoccupied with relationships, usually with members of what truly seemed the "opposite sex." From Frances Whitcher's early-nineteenth-century husband-hunting widows and spinsters to Judith Viorst's struggle to balance feminist beliefs with a desire to be taken care of, problems with men and the need to please them (which in turn spawned humor about dieting and fashion and aging) has assumed a central place in women's humor, even when, as in the work of Marietta Holley at the turn of the century, the woman is clearly the dominant figure. Such relationships are a common theme in *The Best Contemporary Women's Humor* as well, with sections on sex, marriage, men, and motherhood; but the culturally-imposed standards of ideality and perfection have been turned on their heads: no longer do women feel pressure to measure up when men are far from ideal themselves. Dating results in the realization that "There Is No Mr.

Right." And the man in the Martha Campbell cartoon included in the "Hot Spicy Sex" section has managed to bring his sexual partner only to "cloud eight" (and notice who's doing the assessment!).

There's a goodly amount of lesbian humor here, too, which has come *way* up from underground thanks to people such as Kate Clinton and Gail Sausser, who were about the only lesbian writers whose work I could find in the early 1980s. Not only in the "Lydia's Isle" section do we get wry, comic takes on lesbian life, but glimpses are elsewhere, as well, such as in the cartoon by Andrea Natalie in which a child draws her family tree, showing her parents to be "Ma + Mom + New York Sperm Bank."

But clearly these contemporary creators of humorous prose, poetry, and cartoon art are not primarily concerned with relationships. Like most women, they find humor in cats and dogs, work, food, and clothes. Their humor argues for better-designed public restrooms for women, and for greater accessibility for the disabled. There is pro-choice humor, and humor about dreams and therapy.

What's new here, though, is not just the contemporary topicality of much of the humor. These women feel the need to speak from behind traditional roles, and indeed one of the cartoons combines visual and verbal humor to show women quite literally "in" traditional "rolls"—the jelly, the crescent, and so forth. Such freedom to play with visual and verbal images is a hallmark of contemporary women's humor, denoting a sense of security in both being female and being funny. And some aspects of being female are themselves funny. One cartoon queries the training bra: what exactly *does* it train them to do?

There is anger in these pages, too—not covert or subversive, but open and candid shots at limits on women's autonomy. Hattie Gossett takes on the "mins movement," asking what it's for when "aint they still runnin the world?" And Lois Greene Stone points out women's choice between jogging on a boring track and risking a mugging in the park. A Jennifer Berman cartoon goes to the heart of the matter by placing an "Anger Validated Here" table next to one for validating parking tickets. Is anger humorous? It is if you identify with its source. And wasn't Jonathan Swift pretty angry when he wrote "A Modest Proposal"? Shouldn't women be different? The answer in this collection is a resounding NO.

But while much of contemporary women's humor has a clear feminist intent, some of it is just for fun. Flash Rosenberg, as the "Quote Doctor," turns well-known aphorisms inside out, so that the German proverb "Better an empty purse than an empty head" becomes "But an empty bed is going too far." Sabrina Matthews' "The Cat is Not in the Microwave" plays on a familiar urban legend, and a Jennifer Berman cartoon spoofs the PBS series "This Old House" by turning it into a show featuring destructive cats: "Joe is spraying the oriental rug. Let's see how he's doing..."

Who *are* these humorists, anyway? Some of the comic strips, such as Nicole Hollander's "Sylvia," Lynn Johnston's "For Better or For Worse," and Barbara Brandon's "Where I'm Coming From" are nationally syndicated. Shary Flenniken's "Trots and Bonnie" strip appeared in *National Lampoon.* Most of the others will not be as familiar to most readers, which is part of the point of these nearly annual collections that Roz puts together: a lot of women out there are creating humor—humor that disrupts comfortable assumptions and stereotypes, humor that expresses anger and frustration, humor what simply aims to have a good time.

I think you'll have a good time with *The Best Contemporary Women's Humor.*

Nancy A. Walker
Professor, English Dept.
Vanderbilt University

Rina Piccolo

CENSORED EROTICA

by Janice Perry

It was lying beside me, verbing quietly. I could hear its steady breathing and the soft sounds of its verbing. I began to get adjective, so I turned to it and put my body part around it. It looked into my body part and verbed me with its body part. I began to verb and to verb its body part with mine. It moaned and said, "I emotion it when you verb me like that."

There was the sound of its adjective body part rubbing against my body part and the slow rhythm of our verbing each other. It was adverbly verbing me and I began to verb. I saw its color body part and grew more and more emotioned. I know I would soon verb. My skin verbed with excitement, and I felt tiny nouns shooting up and down my body part. I said, "Faster, faster, my endearment, I'm going to verb! Yes, I'm verbing, I'm *verbing*! *verb me*! Oh endearment, you are the *superlative*! I emotion you."

We lay together in silence, and then got up and ate three entire packets of nouns.

Stephanie Piro

"Minimalist? You mean his art... or his lovemaking?"

Stephanie Piro

They were amazed by the success of the "Raw Sex" Booth...

SEXUAL PARAPHERNALIA

by Sara Cytron and Harriet Malinowitz

Do you use sex toys? Well, if you didn't answer that, you're certainly not going to answer this: Do you use sex toys that you can only buy at Acme Hardware? Or Fisher's Surgical Supplies? Or the Police Academy Tag sale? See, it all depends on what kind of role plays you're into.

I once had a girlfriend who was so guilt-ridden about being a lesbian, that the only way she could have an orgasm was if we pretended to be shipwrecked, adrift at sea, far from civilization, never to return. So in order to make this whole thing realistic, I had to buy an inflatable raft, a foot pump, and a bailing bucket.

Plus she lived in New York, I lived in Washington, D.C., and I was always schlepping these things back and forth on the Metroliner.

Then I had a Catholic girlfriend who got off on feeling guilty. So we used to burn frankincense and myrrh while she graphically confessed in my ear everything we were doing.

Then I had another girlfriend who liked sex the best under time pressure—when she had to rush. So we used to pretend that she was an air-traffic controller who had ten seconds to come before two jumbo jets would collide in mid-air. That was exciting—the best nine and a half seconds of my life!

"NOT BAD, HARRY. CLOUD EIGHT."

Martha Campbell

Shary Flenniken

HIGH SCHOOL SEX

by Sibyl James

This term Stout Mama's filling in for a friend who teaches in a small-town high school. Her class is billed as creative writing in the schedule. In high school talk that means elective, a.k.a. nonserious time and an easy A. She has a back row of football players, a huddle of young blonde women teetering on stilt sling-back heels under a load of Revlon, two or three kids who drift in late after a bathroom cigarette. It's spring and balmy enough this week to open the windows to counteract the furnace the school continues to run full blast, and even the one intense poet in the front row hasn't heard a word she's said for two days.

Stout Mama lets the birds win. She tells the students to write whatever comes to mind, and leaves for a cup of tea. Teachers keep only coffee in the faculty pot, so she heads for the home ec room to heat some water in the microwave. Most days the home ec room is fun, more like recess than a class, with a few kids milling around in chocolate chips or pizza dough, the rest of them slouching on tables. Today she walks in on neat rows of seated students with their faces pulled long and chins disappearing into elbows of bored silence. The sex lecture.

Stout Mama remembers her own high school self, remembers sex lectures are ritual, annual as spring. Today, the female home ec teacher sits in back and the school's brought in a man with chalkboard diagrams and a voice sexless as a computer. He's talking about the Whole Person. He has a diagram of circles within circles, inside each circle one piece of the Whole Person: the social piece, the intellectual piece, the physical health piece, the sex piece. He uses words like "component," that sound less racy than "piece."

Stout Mama understands that the diagrams are simply prologue. Everybody knows he's here to talk about the sex piece, that's what he's paid for, but he's setting the scene, building a framework of dull cotton so the kids will be too half-asleep before he gets to facts to snicker. That's what he's really paid for.

Stout Mama slips up the aisle like walking a minefield of suppressed snickers. Not the old-fashioned, fresh-faced embarrassed snicker. These kids live in the late 20th century. Even small towns have cable movies, VCR rentals, and radio stations blasting hits by rap groups. They're laughing at this computer whose program probably reads once a week, Saturday nights after some wine, missionary position.

Stout Mama practices suppressing. She inserts her cup into the microwave and hides behind the chalkboard, waiting for technology to bring her water to a boil.

The prologue's finished. The man announces tonelessly that what he's about to say is simply the facts of it, encyclopedic, and must not be taken as advocating anything. He's ready for the organs. Let's start with the female, he suggests.

Sure. They always start here. Women and children overboard first. Warm up the water before the men get in. Stout Mama grabs her boiling cup and heads for the door. The man has chalked up ovaries and fallopian tubes, and now he's drawing what he refers to as the vaginal canal. Stout Mama wonders briefly if this is a class in obstetrics. Also, states the lecturer, we have the female external genitals. And doesn't draw them.

Stout Mama closes the door and walks back to class, surprising her students, who quickly stub their cigarettes into butts tossed out the window. They've written something in their collective heads: a story about a male rock star who punched a C & W fan senseless in a redneck bar and always sang about sex.

Sex, Stout Mama says, and mentions where

she's been. Her students are seniors; the school believes in preventative maintenance so they heard the ritual last year. The same man. In Stout Mama's class, students feel free not only to snicker, but also groan. They groan.

Well, then you know the one I mean, she grins—the man that draws the ovaries and the fallopian tubes and the vaginal canal and gives up when he gets to the good stuff. The football faces in the back row turn away from the window for the first time this week. She could stick a hatpin in the blondes now and not a one would blink.

Stout Mama turns to the chalkboard. Clitoris, she says. It's something like character motivation or a conflict in the plot. Something you should know about.

They listen past the bell.

Jackie Urbanovic

ENVIRONMENTALLY SAFE SEX

by Cathy Crimmins

FADE IN on gorgeous scene of pine forest; footage of babbling brooks, wildlife shots. Inspiring classical music plays.

NARRATOR (VOICE OVER):
Most Americans want a clean environment. We want to save Planet Earth.

CUT TO scene of a smiling man purchasing a big box of condoms in a drugstore, then later showing them to a woman before he embraces her.

And we're all in agreement that we want to practice safe sex.

The man and woman are "beamed down" into the forest, with little forest creatures staring at them.

But have you ever thought about your ultimate responsibility—Environmentally safe sex?

Man and *woman* look at each other, bewildered. Forest animals scratch their heads.

Yes, now for all the lovers of Planet Earth comes this terrific new video—"Fifty Ways You Can Practice Environmentally Safe Sex."

CUT TO a man in back seat of car with an inflatable doll; he kisses her, she flies out the window.

This educational tape provides dozens of handy tips—#1 Make Sure Your Partner is Biodegradable.

SUPER #1: Make sure your partner is biodegradable.

Gail Machlis

This article says there was a book in the '70s telling women to wrap themselves in Saran Wrap to greet their husbands coming home from work!

People were so ecologically unconscious — then!

machlis

Nicole Hollander

BEING IRRESPONSIBLE

by Flash Rosenberg

One of the most upstanding citizens I know
was telling me he really wants to be a Dad.
So it seemed particularly strange
when he went on to lament
that his girlfriend tells him
he's too irresponsible to have children.
I had to remind him,
"Hey, *Being Irresponsible*
is how most people get kids."

NATURAL FUNCTIONS

by Wendy Lichtman

That there were eighteen boys and two girls in my 12th grade calculus class in 1963 didn't seem odd to us. It was the math class for whiz kids, and we all knew that girls weren't good at math.

I had been good at math in the past, but I was losing it. The reason, according to a Yiddish expression my mother was using a lot lately, was obvious. *When the penis gets hard,* she said, *the brain turns to mashed potatoes.* I figured she must have meant me, but I, of course, had no penis, so I wondered.

David Wolchek was the one responsible for making me lose my mind. He sat across from me in the last seat in row two, and knew, as did I, that calculus was incredibly sexy.

"Why doesn't the asymptote ever really *touch* the hyperbola?" I whispered, holding my hand open to accept the eraser he was returning.

"Infinity," he whispered back, dangling the pink eraser above my palm. "Because x only *approaches* it, but never actually *reaches* it." He grinned, easing the borrowed eraser onto my palm without ever touching me, and we both laughed out loud.

"When the lovebirds in the back of the room finish up," Mr. Ronelli declared, as he continued to write on the blackboard, his back to us, "perhaps we can continue the lesson."

But I barely heard Ronelli's jibe, because I had, at that moment, become aware that something very strange was happening in my quivering body. It seemed that my muscles had begun to melt. They had begun to melt and were apparently seeping out of me into my underpants.

When the penis gets hard, I remembered, looking away from David down to the notebook opened on my desk, *the brain turns to mashed potatoes.* But what about all this, Mother? What the hell is going on here? Where's a Yiddish expression for *me* when I need one?

When I looked up, Mr. Ronelli had swung a full 180 degrees, and was holding his chalk high in the air. "If x lies between 2-1/4 and 2+1/4," he asked suggestively, looking over his wire rims to gaze a moment directly at David, another moment directly at me, "then what are the limits of f(x) when f(x) is 1/2 x+2?"

I stared at his chalk as Mr. Ronelli swung back to write the mathematical symbols on the blackboard. I knew David was watching me, dark eyes smiling. I knew this without looking at him, because I also knew that if I did look at David, more muscle would melt away into my already wet underpants. I pulled my knee socks up to my knees, pulled my skirt down to my knees, and tried to learn the limits Mr. Ronelli was teaching us.

Okay, I asked myself, just how far will this f(x) go on either side? I sketched the graph, did the calculations, and figured it out quicker than anyone else.

No, Mother, it's not my brain. My brain is still okay.

Putting my head down on my folded arms, I closed my eyes and saw my mother's mashed potatoes. A big hot mound on my plate, a little lumpy, salted, topped with a golden pat of butter dripping down the sides, melting from the heat of the potatoes.

Excited, I jerked my head up and turned to a blank sheet in the back of my notebook. I knew I was on the verge of, if not solving the problem, at least framing the question correctly.

$$\frac{\text{vagina}}{\text{penis}} \; \frac{X}{\text{brain}} : \frac{\text{melted butter}}{\text{mashed potatoes}}$$

Heart? Perhaps x is heart, I wondered, looking at my ratio. *As the vagina gets wet, the heart turns to melted butter*. Would that be it? How would it sound in Yiddish?

"Have you solved the problem?" Mr. Ronelli asked, his chalk pointing directly at me.

"No, sir," I said thoughtfully. Then catching my mistake, I quickly corrected it to "Yes, sir," and flipped in my notebook back to the page of the calculus problem.

"When f(x) = 1/2x +2, the limit of f(x) lies between 3-1/8 and 3+1/8," I answered.

"That is perfectly correct. Thank you."

Smiling sweetly, I looked up at Mr. Ronelli. That, I thought, is the easy one.

Amy Sibiga

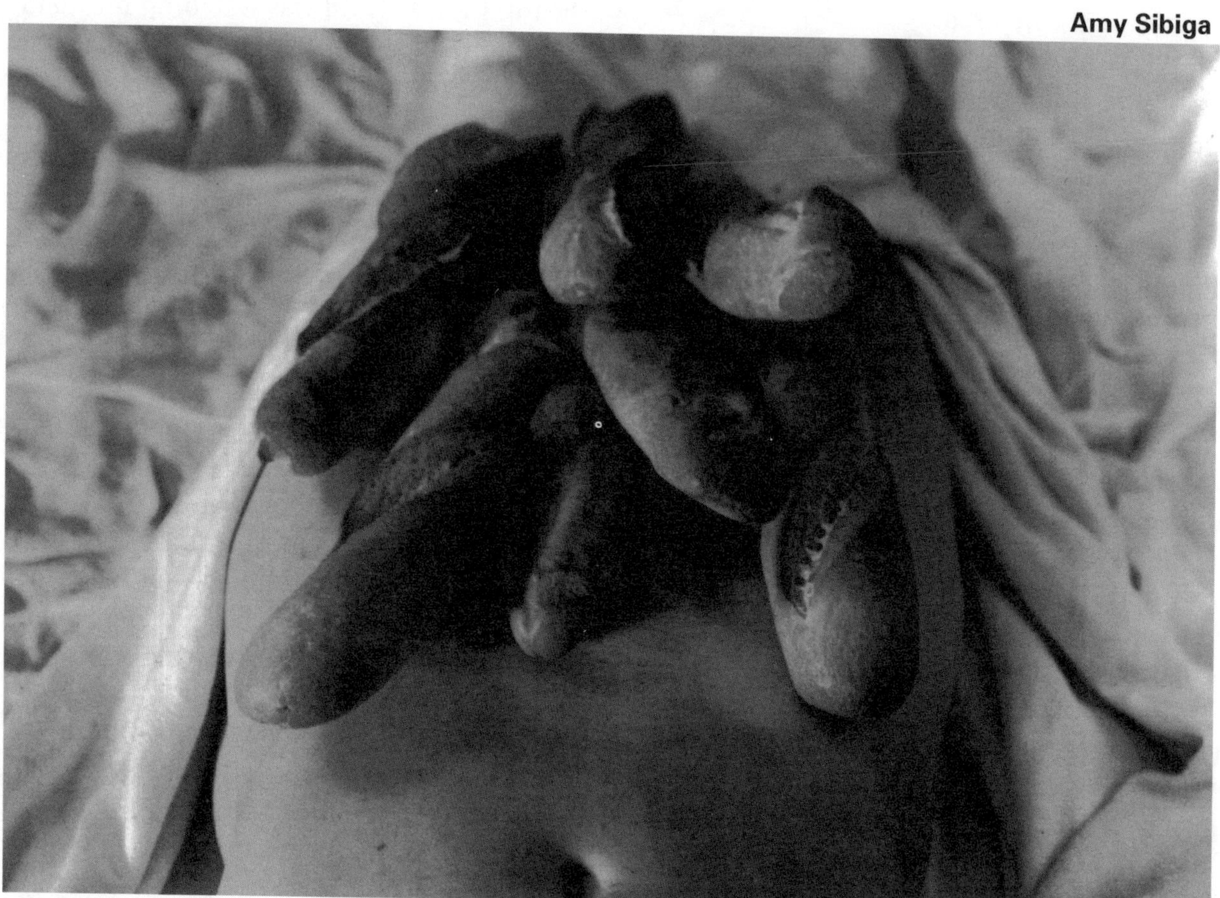

Baguettes

A WAIST IS A TERRIBLE THING TO MIND

Jan Eliot

Gail Machlis

Kathryn Le Mieux

Women in Traditional Rolls

The Crescent

The Jelly

The Hard

The Popover
©lawton

No.56: Little Ones' Lunch

This week, *busy* mature student & mother-of-six, *Wendy Weber*, guides you through the Favourite eating experience of her Under Sevens.....

Menu

Fizzy Drink

Noodles with Sauce

Stew, Mash, Peas

Jelly 'n' ice cream

Chocolate Digestive Biscuit

Wendy and husband, *George*, believe in feeding the younger members of their lively brood, SIMPLE, *balanced* meals.....

Jane Caminos

Rina Piccolo

"... AND LEAD US NOT INTO TEMPTATION, SNACKWISE."

Nicole Hollander

TOMBARBIE AND ME

by Penny S. Lorio

Christmas morning, 1965... Obviously, there was a mix-up at the North Pole. Somewhere in America, a little girl was as puzzled to receive my Erector Set as I was to find her Barbie under my tree. I stared at the doll. It didn't have wheels. There was no place to load a roll of caps. She was simply Barbie—the coveted trophy of plastic femininity. The doll with the perfect complexion, trim figure and long blonde hair...so, what did they expect me to do with it?

"Just use your imagination," Mom advised.

Oh, sure. When I discovered my Easy-Bake oven made a great place to dry worms nobody was real appreciative of my ingenuity.

"You can change her clothes and dress her up to go places," Mom suggested, dumping the accessories out of the box. "Look, here's a comb. You can comb her hair..."

Well, now that promised to be entertaining. I'd have to get up just a little earlier every morning so I could get Barbie ready for the day, before slipping on my overalls and heading out to dig foxholes.

"All girls your age like to play with Barbies," Mom said.

I sensed her disappointment in the fact that I wasn't smitten with the doll. Okay, no pressure. Let me think about this. I picked up the Barbie and looked her over. At least she wasn't one of those dolls that wet her pants. All right, I'd give her a chance. Barbie could travel with me, but she'd have to learn to keep up.

First things first; she'd have to lose the red cocktail dress. Figures, I'd have to spend my Christmas money to buy her a pair of jeans and some sensible shoes. But the last thing I needed when we were hiking through quicksand was to have her gimping along in high heels. And once I got her into some real clothes it didn't take long for my Barbie to begin shedding her glamour-girl image.

My Barbie didn't waste her time going to teas or pool parties. She didn't sit around worrying about whether she'd be asked to the prom. My Barbie had a date with adventure. She was the speedbump in the Driveway 500. She was the first to parachute off the garage. She'd try anything. There wasn't a sissy bone in her body.

Mom didn't understand. Maybe she just wasn't ready to see old stereotypes fall.

"Why is your Barbie in the toilet?" she demanded.

"Scuba training."

She just shook her head. "Get her out of there."

I went into the bathroom and lifted the naked Barbie from the pool. Mom was right on my heels. "Look at that doll," she muttered.

Barbie had been scraped along the ground so much that her tits were getting worn down. Her long, blonde hair was tangled in knots—a big clump was missing in the back. But today she'd set a new underwater record. I was proud of her.

Mom sat down on the edge of the tub. "Let's have a talk."

It seems Mom was concerned that Barbie's behavior was affecting the insects. For some reason, if Barbie continued to snorkel in the toilet, the birds and the bees wouldn't find a flower and there wouldn't be any babies...

Baby whats?

I was confused by all this talk of cross-breeding, and I couldn't understand what the heck any of it had to do with our bathroom.

"So Barbie should start acting like a young lady," Mom explained, reading the dumb expression on my face. "Because someday she's going to meet someone and fall in love. And then she's not going to want to be a tomboy anymore."

Oh, right. Like falling in love was more fun than climbing trees.

"Do you understand what I'm trying to say?" Mom asked.

Of course I did. I wasn't born yesterday. I was seven. I knew about life. "Barbie's already been in love," I said, vouching for the heart of a tomboy.

"Oh, she has?" Mom smiled eagerly. "Does she like Freddy's G.I. Joe?"

I made a face like a person who's been served ketchup on pancakes. "Of course not. Barbie loves Midge..."

Well, now that was a whole different subject.

Dianne Reum

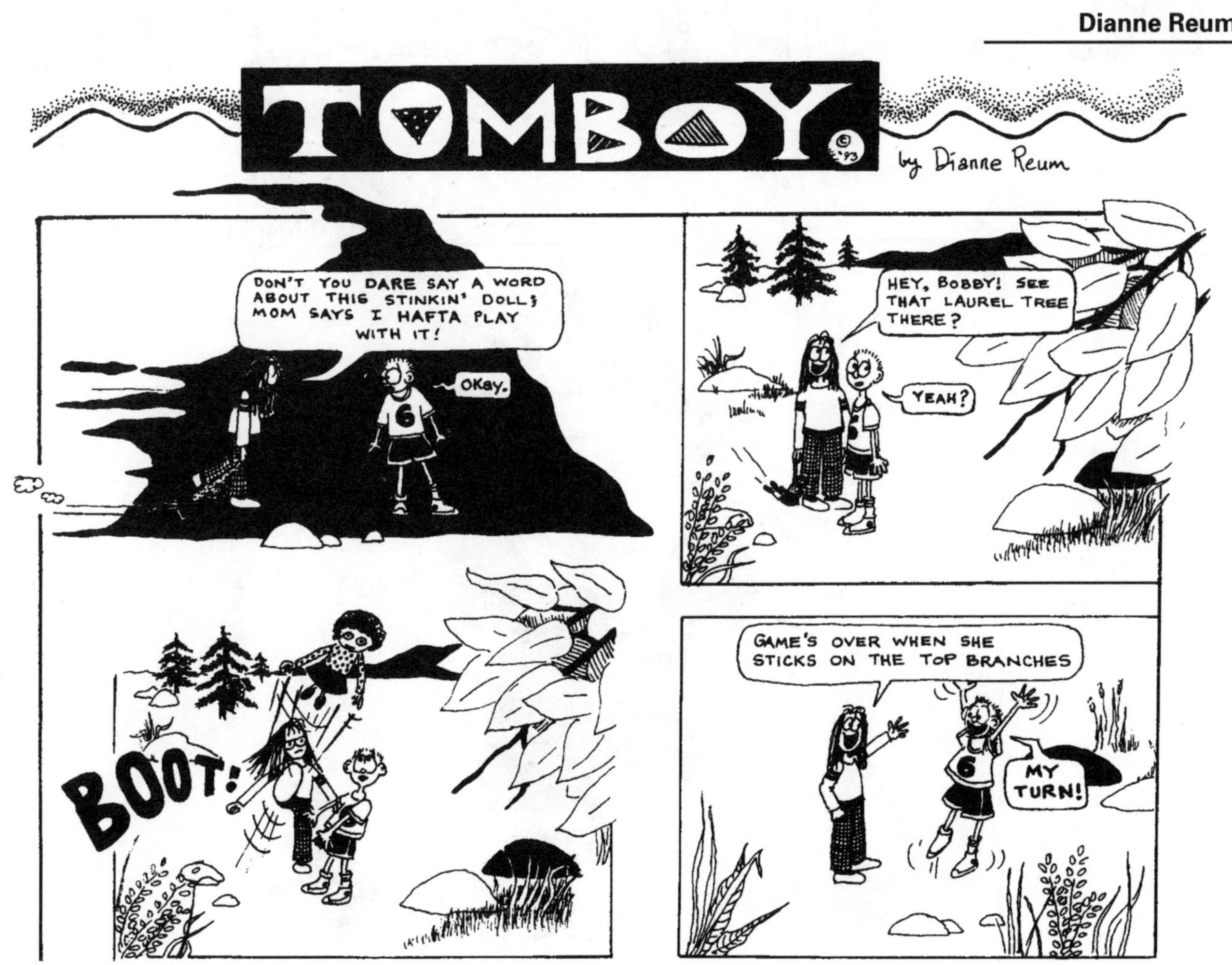

Kathryn LeMieux

Diane DiMassa

Kitty:
Will not use
bathroom
if there is
anyone around
who might
"hear."

Mary Lawton

BATHROOMS

by Sara Cytron and Harriet Malinowitz

My mother and I had all of our major mother-daughter bonding experiences in public bathrooms.

Women—didn't your mother teach you everything you know about public bathrooms?

Remember that first time she taught you how to tear off those little rows of toilet paper so you could line the seat? Because God only knew who had been there before you?

Of course, now that you're an adult, whenever you try it, just when you're almost done lining the seat, some breeze comes along and blows the whole thing all over the floor, right?

Of course, a lot of bathrooms today have these toilet seat covers. But unfortunately, these tissue paper doilies come with no instructions about how to interpret their very ambiguous design. Like, are you supposed to sit there with this big paper tongue hanging beneath you, lolling in the water. Or are you supposed to use it like a Melita coffee filter?

Sometimes, when someone had squat peed and sprayed the seat, your mother would declare a health emergency and make you pee standing up. (Freud said that little girls standing up to pee was evidence of penis envy. I would have liked to see this guy put his ass on a urine-soaked seat, and see how that might have changed psychoanalytic theory.)

So anyway, you're standing up. But even as your leg muscles are holding you in this high crouch position, and your pelvic muscles are trying to relax enough to actually let you pee, under no circumstances can you forget about your bag, because you know if there is no hook on the door, if you put it on the floor even for one second, somebody can easily reach their hand under the door and run off with it. (Has this ever happened to anybody? Do you know anyone who actually lost their bag this way?)

Now one other hazard I don't want to forget to mention is when the lock on the door of the stall is broken, and unless you hold it shut with your hand, it keeps flying back in your face. Or else, everyone who comes into the bathroom figures the stall is empty, and pushes it in your face. ("Oh, sorry! Sorry!")

Of course, you may not have this problem if you happen to get one of those stalls where the hinges are about a mile apart leaving this wide open slit where everybody standing in line can pass the time observing you, until you wish you could charge for pay per view. (Wave) They're all trying to make you feel guilty for taking too much time, so you throw your sweater over the slit.

So there you are, you're standing up, you're holding your bag, you're holding the door closed, and you're trying to keep the top of your pants out of the line of the jet stream all at the same time. But then, you first have to deal with the toilet paper. It's usually at this moment that you realize that you're dealing with one of those flat dispensers that only gives you one little folded square at a time. And of course, they're all jammed up, high inside of it, and you have to break the bones in your fingers to reach inside and pull them down.

Then, have you seen these new high-tech toilet paper dispensers? The kind they have at all the highway rest stops now? Those huge round plastic things, where the manufacturer forgot to put in the teeth that cut the paper? So anytime you try to tear it off, it just keeps coming and coming. You try giving it these little tugs, hoping the paper will just snap off, but it just sets the whole wheel spinning, and the paper comes flying out, till it looks like the whole stall is decorated for somebody's surprise party.

These are just some of the reasons why the line for the women's room is always ten times longer than the line for the men's.

Constance Houck

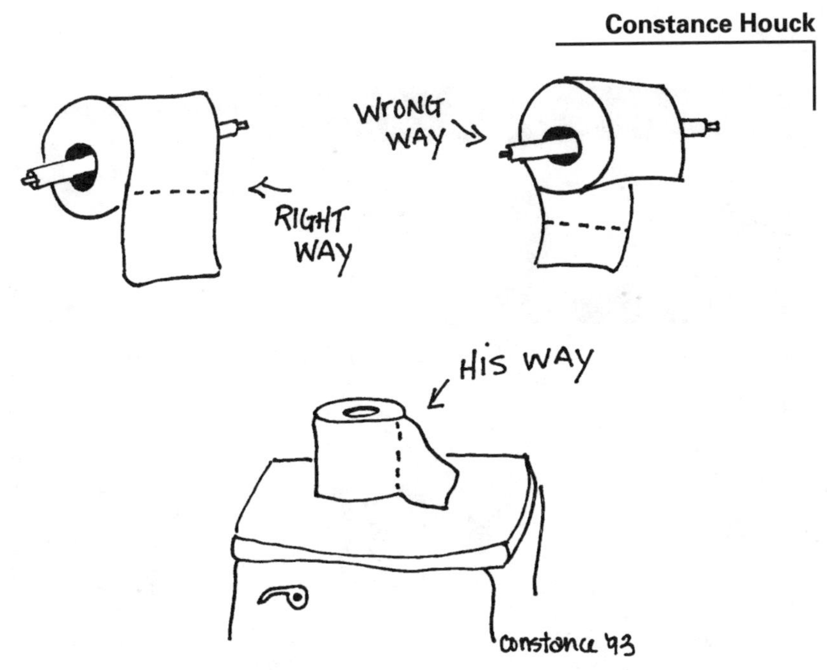

Rina Piccolo

Judy Horacek

Jessica Bruce

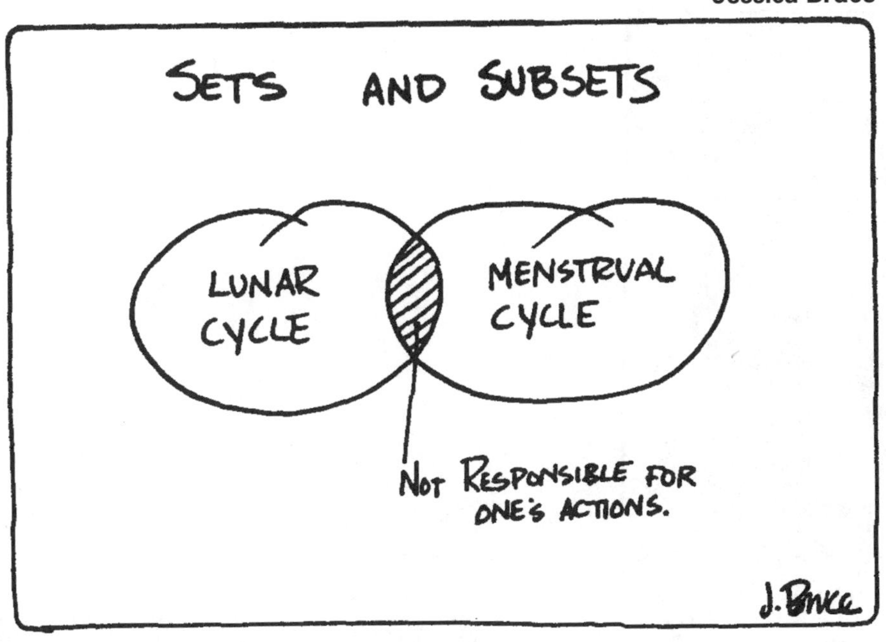

Jane Harty

Jane Goodman

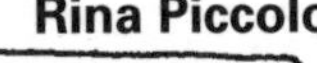
Rina Piccolo

I will never be glamourous
but at least now I know why.

I studied figure drawing
where we learned
well-proportioned adults
are 7 heads tall.

Fashion models are
at least 8 heads tall.
Toddlers are 3 heads tall.
Adolescents about 5.

Seems that
the fewer
heads tall
you are,
the younger
and more comical
you look.

I am only 6 heads tall.

And *THIS* explains
why I turned out so silly.

Though FULLY GROWN
I'm missing a head.

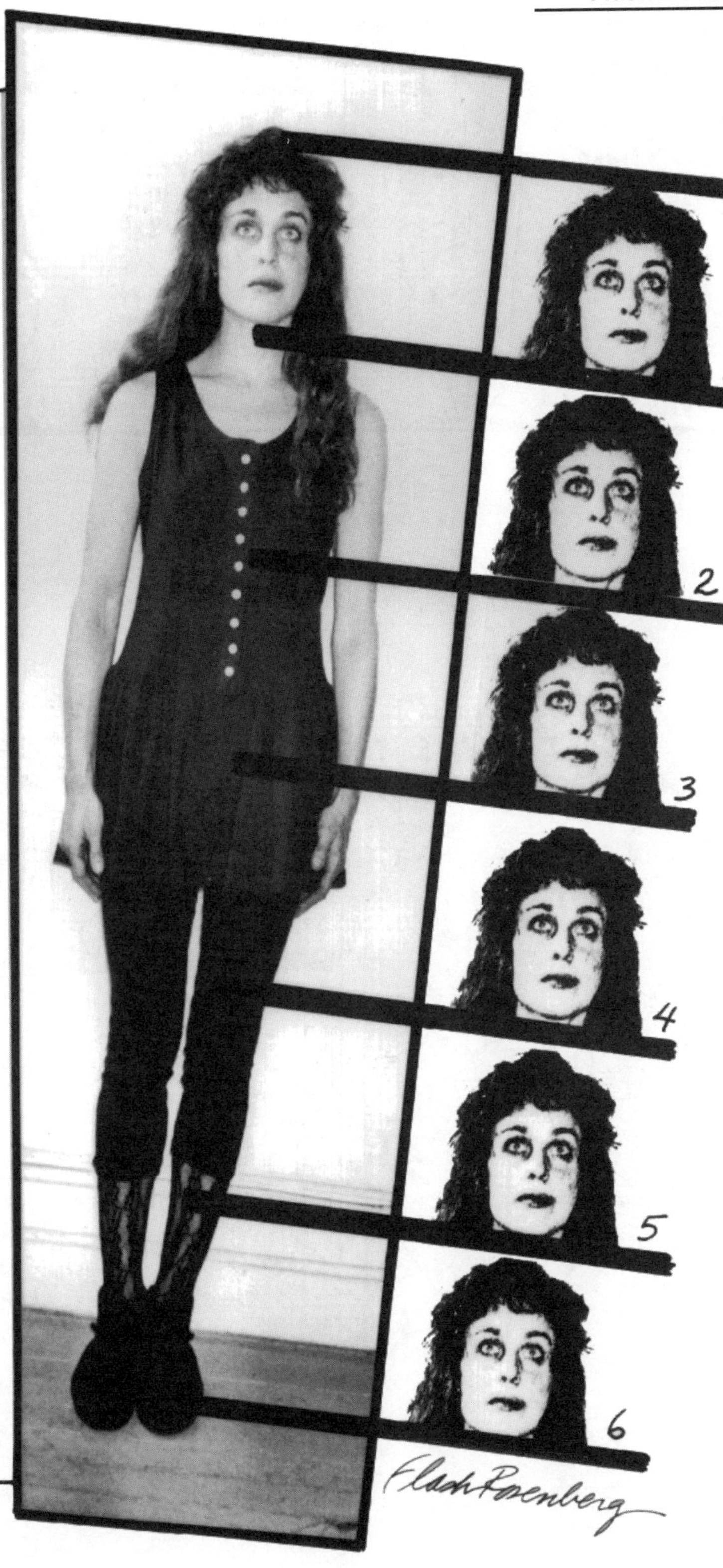

Nicole Hollander

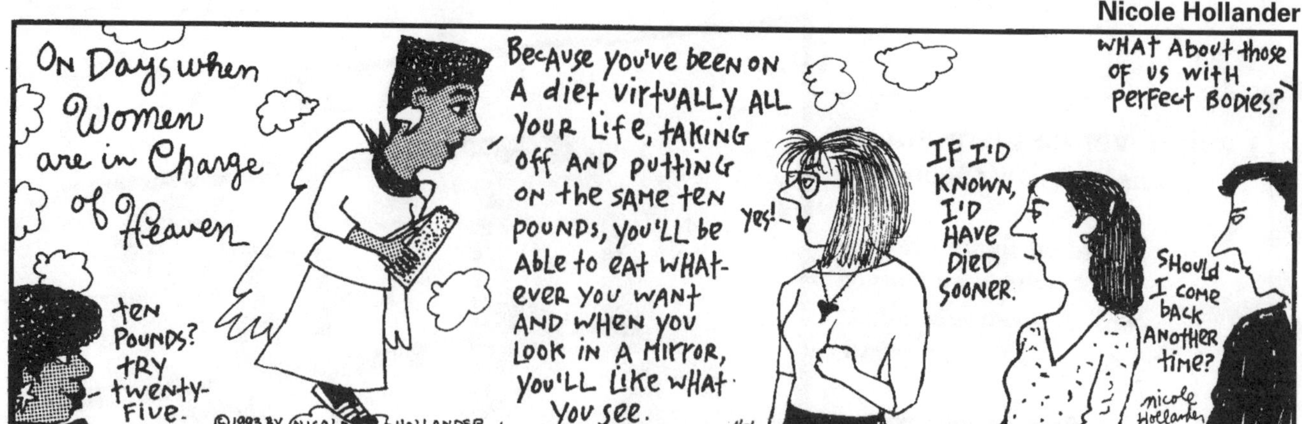

On Days when Women are in Charge of Heaven
Because you've been on A diet virtually all your life, taking off and putting on the same ten pounds, you'll be able to eat whatever you want and when you look in a mirror, you'll like what you see.
Yes!
ten pounds? try twenty-five.
If I'd known, I'd have died sooner.
What about those of us with perfect bodies?
Should I come back another time?
©1993 by Nicole Hollander
4-1
nicole Hollander

Libby Reid

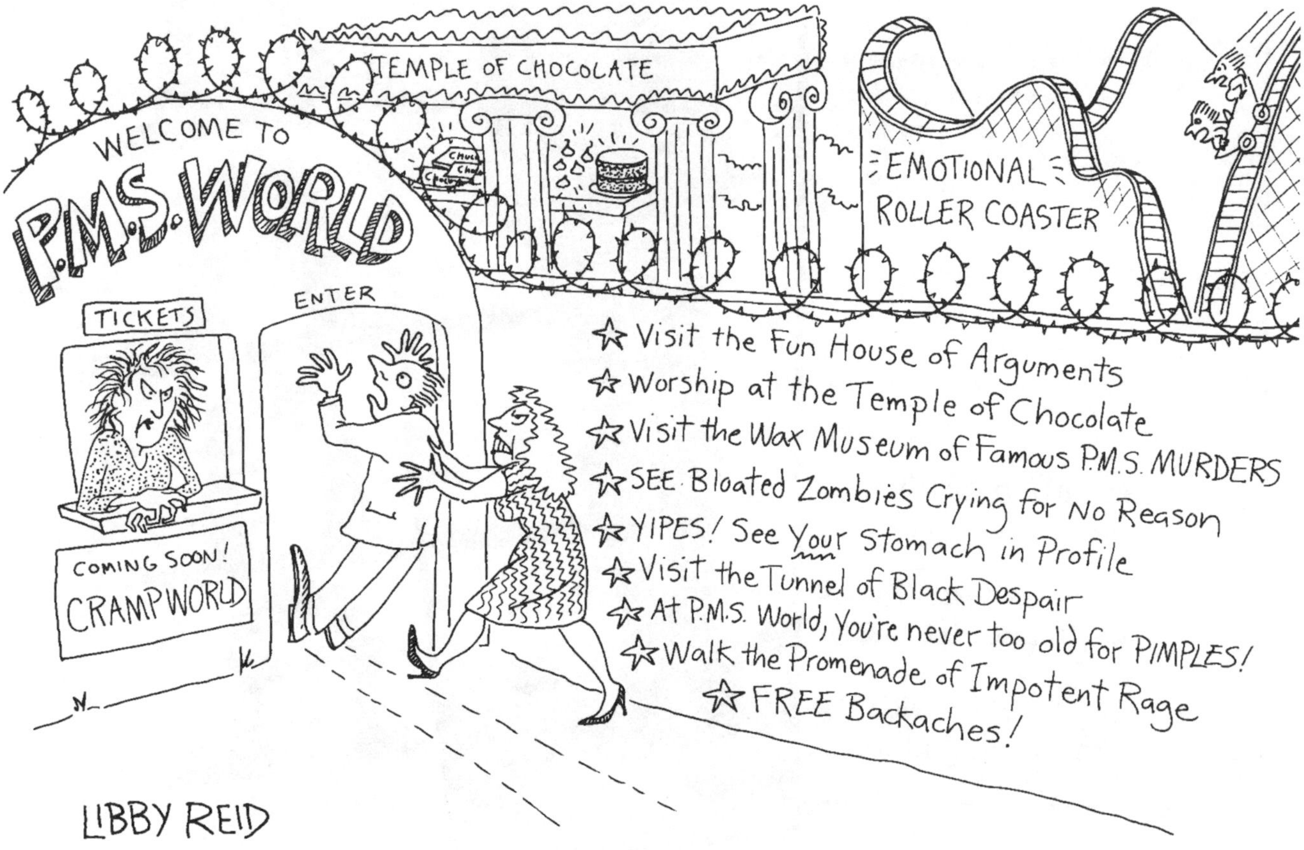
WELCOME TO
P.M.S. WORLD
TEMPLE OF CHOCOLATE
EMOTIONAL ROLLER COASTER
TICKETS
ENTER
COMING SOON! CRAMPWORLD
☆ Visit the Fun House of Arguments
☆ Worship at the Temple of Chocolate
☆ Visit the Wax Museum of Famous P.M.S. MURDERS
☆ SEE Bloated Zombies Crying for No Reason
☆ YIPES! See Your Stomach in Profile
☆ Visit the Tunnel of Black Despair
☆ At P.M.S. World, You're never too old for PIMPLES!
☆ Walk the Promenade of Impotent Rage
☆ FREE Backaches!
LIBBY REID

THOSE HIPS, THOSE THIGHS

Sheree Anne Bradford-Lea

Ever since I reduced my Barbie doll's breasts with my parents' sander I've believed I should help people become all that they can be. Within reason of course. But then there are people like Mr. Henries, a new patient I saw a few days ago. I knew he was trouble when he wouldn't tell my receptionist what his problem was. Women I expect to be shy about plastic surgery—not men. Still, I tried to look unsuspecting as I ushered him to one of my cozy office chairs and sat down behind my desk.

"What can I do for you?" I asked. As I said it I couldn't resist playing a guessing game. At first glance Rhinoplasty seemed the most obvious—and maybe the ears—

Mr. Henries cleared his throat. "I want bigger hips and thighs."

"I beg your pardon?" I said.

"I want hips and thighs. You know, like a woman's," he said.

I smiled. "Oh, I see, you're a transsexual," I said. "That's fine, but you don't really need surgery—you have an androgynous female look already. Sure, you'll never have an hourglass figure but—"

"No, no, I'm not a transsexual," Mr. Henries said.

"Well then, you've got me," I said. "Why would you want a woman's figure if you don't want to be a woman?"

"I think the female body is beautiful. I'm sick of having no hips and skinny thighs. And my butt! It's small, and tight, and—I just can't bear the sight of it in the mirror."

"Are you sure you're not a transsexual?" I said. "Believe me, it's all right to admit it if you are. Really."

"Damn it!" Mr. Henries shouted. "Stop trying to make me into something I'm not!"

"All right, I'm sorry," I said, leaning back in my chair. "But have you thought of the disadvantages? Besides the surgical risks, that is."

The man looked at me. "What disadvantages?"

He had me there. I coughed, trying to buy time. Then I had it. "You might have trouble fitting into clothes, you know. Men's clothing wasn't made for hips."

"Well—" Mr. Henries said.

"And what about the fact that if your hips and thighs are bigger, that'll make your chest look smaller. You might need surgery to alter that—"

"You mean chest implants?"

"Yes, that's more surgery. See? You unbalance one thing surgically and you might need more surgery to balance things up again. So maybe you should think about it and *then* maybe come back—"

"You're just trying to get rid of me!"

"No, no, I don't think you've thought of all the angles here, that's all."

"That's where you're wrong," he said. "What's important is that I feel good about my body."

"Well, yes," I said, "But—I've got to tell you, the kind of thing you're talking about—there isn't a procedure currently available—"

"That's why I came to you. You advertise that you offer innovative new treatments. So don't you?"

"Well, yes, but—"

"Then make one for me. Give me hips and thighs and a larger butt."

I straightened in my chair so I'd look taller. "No," I said firmly.

Mr. Henries straightened up too. "Why not?" he asked grimly.

"I don't want to. It's unnatural."

"That's rich, coming from *you*."

"Well, it's my choice. I don't have to explain

myself to you."

"Alright," Mr. Henries said, his voice shaking with anger. "Then give me the name of another doctor."

"Fine," I said, scribbling down the name of a person who owed me money. "Try her then." Mr. Henries snatched the paper out of my hand, turned and left the office.

I breathed a sigh of relief. Then the buzzer sounded and my receptionist informed me I had another new patient, a Ms. Jonas. She wouldn't state her problem either. As I showed Ms. Jonas to Mr. Henries' vacated seat I surreptitiously studied her and figured Rhinoplasty was a definite bet here.

"So, what can I do for you?" I asked, trying to sound cheerful.

"Liposuction," she said softly, desperately. "Doctor, I have to get rid of these hips, these thighs. They're enormous. And my butt—I can't bear the sight of it in the mirror."

I smiled, happy again. It was good to have things back to normal.

Viv Quillin

Mary Lawton

Gail Machlis

Jane Caminos

Lynn Johnston

For Better or For Worse
By Lynn Johnston

Shary Flenniken

Trots and Bonnie

BONNIE!
YOUR HIPS ARE BEGINNING TO STICK OUT!
WHAT YOU NEED IS A GOOD WORK OUT TO TONE THOSE THIGHS.

IF YOU BUILD UP YOUR SHOULDERS, YOUR HIPS WILL LOOK SMALLER!

OKAY... NOW TOUCH YOUR TOES!

IF YOU DO THIS ENOUGH, YOU WON'T GROW OLD AND DIE.

SWEAT OUT ALL THE POISONS IN YOUR BODY AND WASH THEM AWAY.

NOW!
CLOSE THOSE PORES AND **FREEZE THEM SHUT!**

WE'LL BEAT THE BACON OFF!

IF ALL ELSE FAILS, TAN FLAB PASSES FOR MUSCLE.

INCREDIBLE PROGRESS! YOU'RE ALREADY SHOWING RESULTS!
YOU MEAN THESE BRUISES?

NOW YOU CAN REWARD YOURSELF WITH THIS RAW-CABBAGE SALAD.
IT'S HARD TO CHEW.
THAT'S THE POINT.... IT PASSES THROUGH YOUR BODY WITHOUT BEING DIGESTED.

THIS BEN-GAY IS SOAKING INTO MY PAW PADS.
RUB HARDER, TROTS. I'VE GOT TO GET UP AT FIVE A.M. SO I CAN BICYCLE FIFTY MILES BEFORE SCHOOL STARTS.

BY THE WAY... YOU'RE LOOKING A LITTLE PUDGY YOURSELF.... WHY DON'T YOU JOIN ME?
NO THANKS. I'M PLANNING TO SLEEP IN AND EAT YOUR BREAKFAST.

SHARY FLENNIKEN

BAR BAR

Roz Chast

Karen Favreau

I'm the typical star of your typical beer ad: male, white, age 28-34 and likeable in that Bruce Willis/ frat boy kind of way: I dig fast cars, fast chicks and ROCK N' ROLL!

NY

NIKE

I'm the typical FEMALE in the typical beer ad. I almost never DRINK beer. Instead, I SERVE it to men in rowdy sports bars.

Sometimes I magically appear in a bathing suit when some-one cracks open a brewski.

"Hey babe! Hubba Hubba!"

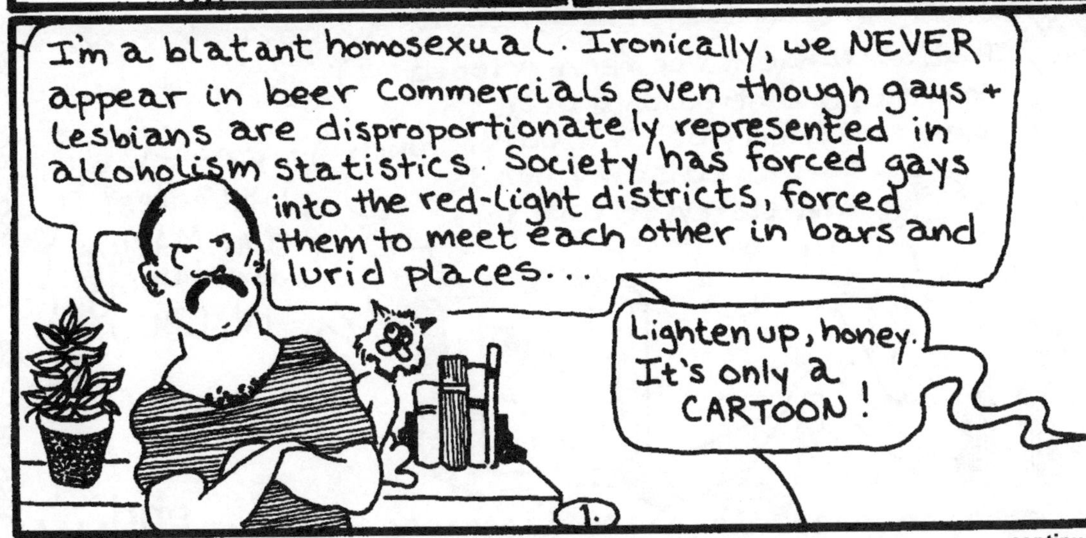

continued...

I'm the original party animal. Scantily-clad babes used to fawn over me. I'm bitter because I was exploited and because JOE THE CAMEL is more popular than me.
I'm one of those subliminal images that flashes across the screen or is camouflaged in the ice cubes. I make things like going for a drive after drinking a case of beer seem appealing.
MR. THANATOS
CONSUME
DEATH
SEX
Drink
Recovering alcoholic with 20 days clean trying to watch a football game.
God...grant me the serenity...
it's time to sit through ANOTHER flashy Beer commercial America!
I'm an aging rock star. My latest tour is sponsored by a major beer company even though 2 of my old musician chums drank themselves to death in the 70's. I'm also gay, but I married a gorgeous model so no one will figure it out. JUST SAY NO TO DRUGS, KIDS!!
That's strange... I've been gripped by this uncontrollable urge to get smashed, belch loudly, crunch a can against my head and listen to bad rock music.
Hi Ladies! I'm MAXINE the dancing MAXI PAD!
2.
end.

Nicole Hollander

FAMILY VALUES

Andrea Natalie

Barbara Brandon

Andrea Natalie

Roz Chast

MORE NONTRADITIONAL FAMILY UNITS

Guy, Chair, Three-Way Lamp

A Woman, Her Daughter, Forty-four My Little Ponies

The Troy Triplets and Their Personal Trainer

Two Guys, Two Gals, Two Phones, a Fax, and a Blender

R. Chast

ACCESSIBILITY

Angela Martin

ONE AFTERNOON IN THE
GROVES OF ACADEME
©1988 BY ALISON BECHDEL
31
PLANNING HAS BEGUN FOR THE ANNUAL GAY & LESBIAN STUDIES CONFERENCE.
COMMITTEES HAVE BEEN FORMED.
CLARICE IS ON HER WAY TO THE FIRST MEETING OF THE ACCESSIBILITY COMMITTEE.
GINGER, GRADUATE STUDENT IN ENGLISH, LEAVES HER SECTION OF FRESHMEN WITH SOME WORDS OF WISDOM...
QUIT WHINING! READING SOMETHING BY SOMEONE WHO'S NOT STRAIGHT, WHITE, & MALE IS NOT GOING TO KILL YOU!
AND SETS OUT FOR THE VERY SAME MEETING.
WE NEED TWO PEOPLE TO TAKE THIS WHEELCHAIR AND MAKE SURE THESE WORKSHOP LOCATIONS ARE REALLY ACCESSIBLE.
OUR WIMMIN VOLUNTEER!
MY NAME'S CLARICE. I'M AT THE LAW SCHOOL. YOU'RE ONE OF LOIS' HOUSEMATES, RIGHT?
YEAH. I'M GINGER. I'VE SEEN YOU AROUND BUT WE'VE NEVER MET.
UH-UH.
NOPE.
YOUR TURN. I'M GETTING BLISTERS.
DAMN.
THIS IVORY TOWER NEEDS SOME RAMPS!
WHAT ARE YOU SAYING, GINGER?! BUILD RAMPS AND ANYONE COULD GET UP!! THE WHOLE SCHOOL WOULD BE OVERRUN BY BLACK COMMIE DYKES IN WHEELCHAIRS! REALLY, NOW!

Cath Jackson

Cinders McLeod

...A ROLLING DONUT
©1991 BY ALISON BECHDEL
124
MORNING.
HI, MO.
LOIS, WHAT'S WITH THEA? I MEAN, WHY'S SHE IN A WHEELCHAIR?
I DUNNO. WHY DONCHA ASK HER?
BIG NEW BOOK!
YEAH. I KNOW IT'S HARD TO BELIEVE, MO, BUT THE WHEELCHAIR DOESN'T IMPAIR MY HEARING AT ALL.
ECONOMIC FORECAST DEEP DOO DOO
DONUT HUT
UH... SORRY. I WAS JUST WONDERING WHY YOU'RE.. YOU KNOW... USING THAT IF NORMALLY YOU JUST USE CRUTCHES.
WELL THE CHAIR IS SO MUCH MORE DRAMATIC, DON'T YOU THINK? I USE IT WHEN I WANT PEOPLE TO FEEL EXTRA SORRY FOR ME.
PHEW! MAGIC JOHNSON ISN'T ONE OF THEM
A TIP O' THE NIB TO ZANA
UH...
HEY, I'M JUST KIDDING YOU. I'M REALLY USING THE CHAIR TODAY BECAUSE IT GOES SO GREAT WITH MY SHOES.
NO, SERIOUSLY. THE REAL REASON IS BECAUSE I TOOK MY CRUTCHES INTO THE SHOP FOR REPAIRS AND THEY WERE ALL OUT OF LOANERS! IT WAS THIS CHAIR OR A '76 HONDA!
THEA, I'M SORRY I...
NO! NO! THAT'S NOT IT! I'M USING THE CHAIR BECAUSE I TORE A HOLE IN THE SEAT OF MY PANTS THIS MORNING AND I DIDN'T HAVE TIME TO MEND IT! HA HA HAW!
HATE CRIMES UP
BUCHANAN/DUKE POSSIBLE TEAM—'92
WOMEN'S GLIB
SLAP!
OKAY, OKAY—HEH HEH—FOR REAL NOW. I GET FATIGUED A LOT. ON BAD DAYS I USE THE CHAIR SO I HAVE MORE ENERGY FOR MY WORK AND STUFF.
YOU MUST BE EXHAUSTED AFTER THAT LITTLE ROUTINE. WANT A DONUT?
THEA, DON'T EAT THOSE! THEY'RE FULLA SUGAR AND GREASE! POISON!
OH, BUT IT'S OK FOR LOIS TO HAVE THEM? I JUST LOVE WHEN ABLE-BODIED WOMEN GIVE ME NUTRITIONAL ADVICE.
DON'T TAKE IT PERSONALLY, THEA. SHE SAID THE SAME THING TO ME 4,000 TIMES. IGNORE HER AND EVENTUALLY SHE GIVES UP.
D'YOU HAVE ANY OF THOSE ONES WITH TOXIC-LOOKING SPRINKLES?

The Struggle continues
We think you are marvellous
So patient
Mind the lady

THERE IS NO MR. RIGHT!

Bonnie Timmons

Underutilized Ice-Breakers

Roz Chast

A SERIOUS PERSON

by Wendy Cope

I can tell you're a serious person
And I know from the way you talk
That what goes on inside your head
Is pure as the whitest chalk.

It's nice to meet serious people
And hear them explain their views:
Your concern for the rights of women
Is especially welcome news.

I'm sure you'd never exploit one;
I expect you'd rather be dead;
I'm thoroughly convinced of it—
Now can we go to bed?

Mary Lawton

Nina Paley

Marian Henley

I feel like I've Known you forever, Simone!
I feel the same way about you!

It's so hard to meet people you can trust right away!
Or people willing to trust you in RETURN!

We live in such CYNICAL times!
So. Would you like to get together AGAIN?

Yes!
Then I want you to meet someone SPECIAL...

Someone I wouldn't introduce to just ANYBODY!
GASP You mean you brought...

My lawyer!
Upon concluding these informal negotiations...
I brought mine, too!
"In the event that either party defaults..."
© 1993 Marian Henley

DATING LIKE CLOTHES SHOPPING
by Flash Rosenberg

Imagine if we had to shop for clothes by candlelight
and would be stuck trying on *only one outfit*
for about four hours.
Sounds crazy, doesn't it?
So why is this the system we use for dating?
Dating should be more like clothes shopping.
Surely, finding someone to love is lots more important than any dress.
Instead of wasting so much time going out for dinners,
it'd be more sensible to go to a cramped room with *big* mirrors and harsh lighting,
where we'd be allowed to try on up to six guys at a time.
There'd be a saleswoman on duty to advise us,
while making sure no one steals anybody.
Then without any hassle, she can simply put back the guys that don't fit.

Barbara Brandon

Nina Paley

"RELATIONSHIPS." WHAT A TIRED, OLD, WORN-OUT TOPIC.
PHOOEY!
NINA WOULD FORGET ABOUT THEM ALTOGETHER IF IT WEREN'T FOR PEOPLE SMOOCHING EVERYWHERE SHE LOOKS.
SLURP!
SLOBBER
DROOL
DISGUSTING...
...I WISH I WERE DOING THAT...
EVEN NOW, NINA'S BRAIN LEAPS ABOUT, WONDERING HOW SHE'S GOING TO GET THE RELATIONSHIP OF HER DREAMS.
CUT THAT OUT!
WONDER WONDER PONDER PONDER WONDER WONDE
BOING!
BOING!
LEAP!
EXPERIENCE WOULD SUGGEST THERE IS NOTHING YOU CAN DO TO "MAKE" A RELATIONSHIP HAPPEN. AT LEAST NOT THE KIND OF RELATIONSHIP YOU WANT. YET NINA ALWAYS WONDERS, IS IT REALLY OUT OF HER CONTROL? DO THESE THINGS REALLY JUST HAPPEN ON "GOD'S TERMS"??
You bet your ass, honey.
VOICE O' GOD
NINA HAS THIS NAGGING FEAR THAT SHE WILL EVENTUALLY GET INTO A ROMANTIC RELATIONSHIP, BUT WITH SOMEONE SHE DOESN'T LIKE.
SIGH ALL THOSE CUTE GUYS AROUND. TOO BAD I'M STUCK WITH MONDO HERE. OH WELL, "BEGGARS CAN'T BE CHOOSERS."
SO WHY DOES NINA YEARN FOR A RELATIONSHIP WHEN SHE KNOWS WHAT A PAIN THEY ARE?
YEARN
CRAVE
YEARN
CUZ YOU'RE A DUMBSHIT!
VOICE O' NEGATIVITY
MAYBE IT'S DUE TO THOSE PESKY HORMONES EXERCISING THEIR POWER...
GO ON! HUP! GET YERSELF A MAN!
HEY!
HORMONES
...OR PERHAPS IT'S DUE TO THE DEEP YEARNINGS OF NINA'S "CHILD WITHIN" FOR PATERNAL LOVE.
WAAAA! I WANT DADDY!!!
SHUT UP! WOULD YOU SHUT UP!?
NINA HASN'T QUITE COME TO TERMS WITH ALL THESE FORCES AT WORK WITHIN HER, AND SO SHE FEELS A LITTLE STRAINED...
STRAIN!
STRAIN!
UURRGHH..
...BUT SHE KNOWS THERE'S NO POINT IN TRYING TO TELL HER HEART WHAT TO DO.
LOOK, I'M DRIVIN' THIS TRAIN, SO QUIT HASSLING ME!
NINA THINKS THERE'S GOT TO BE AN ANSWER TO ALL THESE RELATIONSHIP DILEMMAS. WHAT'S THE @*?#!! ANSWER?!
OH GOD NO, NOT THAT!!
THE END?

Flash Rosenberg

Carol Lay

STORY Minute © 1992 CAROL LAY
"THE MANLY MAN"

SHE HEARD THAT A GUY SHE KNEW WAS INTERESTED IN A DATE SO SHE ASKED ABOUT HIM.

HIS FAVORITE ACTOR IS JOHN WAYNE AND HE LIKES HIM IN "THE QUIET MAN" QUITE A LOT.

SHE COULD SEE WHY HE IDENTIFIED WITH THE DEAD DUKE..

TALL
SANDY HAIR
BLUE EYES
MACHO
DETERMINED SMOKER

..BUT WAS **SHE** A SUITABLE MAUREEN O'HARA?

..NOT EVEN CLOSE...

SHE IMAGINED HOW THE STORY WOULD FIT SCENIC CULVER CITY.

OW! HEY!

C'MON, WOMAN!

HE COULD DRINK LIKE AN IRISHMAN JUST AS WELL HERE AS ANYWHERE ELSE, SHE SUPPOSED...

URP!

..BUT HER BROTHER WAS ON THE EAST COAST SO THAT PART WAS OUT.

CRACK!

I'LL LAY YE AMONG THE SWEE' PEAS! ACK-ACK-ACK!

BESIDES, SHE JUST WASN'T MUCH OF THE HOUSEWIFE TYPE.

WOMAN! BRING ME MY SUPPER!

GET IT YOURSELF, ASSHOLE.

Lynda Barry

"TRUTH IS: TELL ME DO YOU LIKE ME. DARE IS: I DARE YOU TO TELL ME DO YOU LIKE ME." YOU DON'T KNOW BOYS I TELL HER BUT SHE GIVES HIM THE LETTER ANYWAY WITH A PERFECT DRAWING ON IT OF A DADDY ROTH RACE CAR. KEVIN'S FAVORITE. "ART IS GOOD FOR THINGS" SHE SAYS.

IF YOU CAN BELIEVE IT THE ANSWER OF KEVIN IS YES. YES HE LIKES MARLYS BUT ITS A LET'S MAKE A DEAL. DOOR NUMBER ONE IS SHE HAS TO KEEP IT SECRET. DOOR NUMBER TWO IS SHE HAS TO KEEP MAKING HIM DRAWINGS. AND DOOR NUMBER THREE IS HE GETS TO TELL PEOPLE IT WAS HIM WHO MADE THE DRAWINGS.

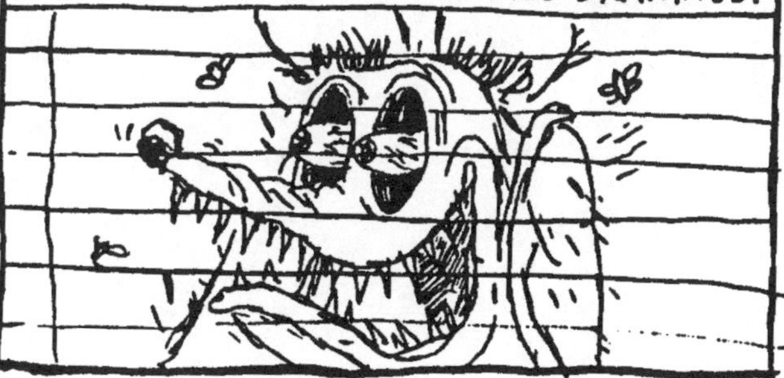

WORTH IT! SHOUTS MARLYS. WORTH IT WORTH IT WORTH IT TO THE MILLIONTH POWER! YOU CAN SEE HER RIGHT NOW BENDING OVER THE PAPER AND DRAWING. SNEAKING OUT OF BED AT NIGHT AND DRAWING THE PICTURES FOR KEVIN TURNER ALWAYS LEAVING THE PERFECT SPOT EMPTY FOR WHERE HE CAN SIGN HIS NAME.

WHAT NOT TO SAY TO AN INDIAN GIRL

by Mina Kumar

1) Why do Indian women wear red dots on their foreheads?

The painful fact is, that's where we menstruate. This question has been asked by everyone I have ever slept with, to the point that I think that people sleep with me only to discover the answer to this ancient Indian secret.

2) Your English is excellent.

I usually reply, "So is yours." This puts a prompt end to the conversation.

3) Do you know a good guru?

4) I am very interested in Sanskrit philosophy.

Said by a Florentine while his hand was up my skirt. It made my mind wander from the events at hand to the nature of imperialism, so I can safely say that it diminishes sexual ardor.

5) Why do you speak English so well?

6) Does your father wear a turban?

7) I am sure you will be able to help India's starving masses after you get your degree from a Western university.

I have heard this over and over again. I usually reply, "Yes, it's a fair exchange. My sister is aiding the West's starving masses with her degree from ITT."

8) How did you learn to dance like a black girl?

a) Because I was kidnapped by the dancers on "Solid Gold" when I was an infant.

b) Because I am really a black girl in disguise.

c) Because Dravidians are actually Africans sent to colonize South Asia.

9) What caste are you?

Of course, it's worse when Indians ask this.

10) What tribe are you from?

11) I bet you like spicy food.

Actually, I subsist on grits and Spam.

12) You guys are good at physics.

Not said by anyone who knows me personally. Or by anyone who has any chance of getting to know me better...

Use any opening line but these and the Indian girl of your choice will faint with gratitude into your arms.

TROTS AND BONNIE
WHY DON'T YOU CALL HIM?
IT'S SO HARD TO THINK OF WHAT TO SAY.
IF I WAS INCREDIBLY BEAUTIFUL, I WOULDN'T HAVE TO SAY ANYTHING.
THERE'D BE SO MANY BOYS AROUND, I'D BE TRIPPING OVER THEM ON MY WAY TO ANSWER THE PHONE.
I COULD PICK AND CHOOSE THE ONES I LIKED BEST.
THEY'D DO ANYTHING FOR ME, JUST TO BE NEAR MY GORGEOUS BODY.
THEY'D TAKE CARE OF ME. THEY'D TREAT ME LIKE A PRINCESS.
THEY'D TOUCH ME AND STROKE ME AND MAKE ME FEEL GOOD.
ALL I'D HAVE TO DO IS SIT THERE AND BE ADORABLE.
SOUNDS PRETTY MUCH LIKE BEING A DOG.
I GUESS THAT MEANS I'LL HAVE TO DEVELOP A PERSONALITY.
HEY, NELSON. HOW DO YOU FEEL ABOUT AGGRESSIVE WOMEN?
NOW ASK HIM IF HE WANTS TO TIP OVER SOME GARBAGE CANS AND THEN GO FOR A ROMP IN THE PARK.
©83 SHARY FLENNIKEN

Jan Eliot

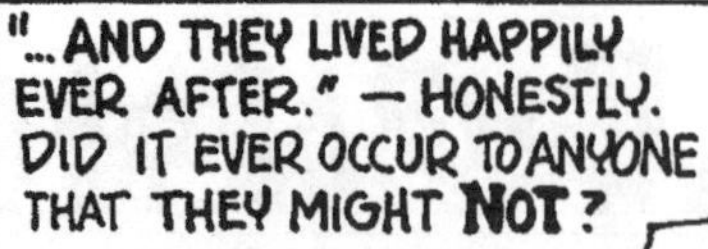

Nicole Hollander

Theresa Henry Smith

Mary Lawton

Mary Lawton

Roz Chast

HOW ABOUT A REFILL ON THAT COFFEE?

by Stephanie Brush

Poor Kyle McLaughlin. Now it appears he's agreed to take the role of Agent Cooper in the upcoming "Twin Peaks" movie after all. He's accepted the reality that for the rest of his acting life, he will unstintingly be identified with the line, "*Damn* that's good coffee. And *hot*."

How can anyone go uphill from that? Is there anything that really cuts to the heart & soul, and capillaries, of the human condition *more* than an outstanding morning cup of coffee?

Is there a time in your life when you feel more fully alive than after that first 1,000-volt jolt in the morning? When you find yourself doing a little drugged hula of delight over something as simple as watching the Weather Channel?

According to the New York Times, "Caffeine is the most widely used psychoactive substance on Earth." Just a fancy way of saying, "World's most popular *drug*." We just get all namby-pamby about calling it that.

Scientists are constantly feeding little cups of coffee to rats ("Cream or sugar, Herman? *Don't bite!!*") trying to figure out exactly how it does affect the brain, so they can report back to us about whether we should feel guilty about not giving it up.

Let's face it: If it's good coffee-news, we tape it up to the refrigerator. If it's bad news, we wad it up and throw it away wrapped around the Mocha Java grounds.

Lately the news seems mostly good: Actual scientists from Johns Hopkins University have stated in print that caffeine "enables people to work harder and think more clearly." Also, it may play a role in "setting the body's biological clocks and in warding off depression."

I think that if they study this further they'll find that in fact depressed coffee-drinkers are still depressed—they're just too busy dancing around the kitchen playing air-guitar at 9 a.m. to notice.

I tend toward depression, myself. My ex-boyfriend Bob had a name for me after I'd had my coffee: "Ed Grimley." This was the character Martin Short used to play on "Saturday Night Live": innocent, hyper-wired demented, Pollyanna-ish.

As a diehard coffee-addict, I am all those things for exactly 1 1/2 hours a day. For a tiny morsel of the morning, I have the personality of a morning disc jockey. For the rest of the day, I have the personality of a pot roast.

Yes, one of the amazing things about coffee is the range of almost-mythological emotions it evokes, depending on the time of day you drink it: The morning cup of coffee is about new beginnings—the rooster crowing, the eggs frying in the pan, the morning paper. The afternoon cup of coffee is more reflective. Friendly, mellowly re-energizing.

Then there's that Late Night Splash of Joe—probably the mournfullest beverage ever invented.

People drinking coffee late at night are a sad bunch—like in that famous Edward Hopper painting "Nighthawks"; a line of stony-faced misfits, needing to stay awake in the darkness for some god-forsaken reason. Laboratory rats given coffee late at night often request to hear old Patsy Cline recordings, and they stare off into the distance thinking of Lost Rat-Loves, lost Rat-Opportunities. OK, maybe I'm joking. Although they do play little rat-harmonicas when the scientists aren't looking. "I like it black," they say to each other. "I like it strong. What, in the end, is rat-life?"

I have tried to give up "real" coffee for de-caf many, many times. But it's sort of like wearing fake jewelry, or having a bogus car phone. You just don't get any bang for your buck. De-caf represents the wimpification of America.

Just as I think we are getting back to red meat, and Traditional Family values, and big cars, and pro-wrestling, we will, eventually, nationally, turn our backs on de-caf.

Also, tea. I mean, *tea*? Puh-leeze.

I remember the first time I visited Canada with my parents, which, I may point out, still has pictures of the Queen of England on its money. As we sat in a diner, the waitress came up with a steaming pot. "Tea?" she said.

"Oh, my God," my Dad said. "This is another *country*."

Luckily, we made it back over the border in time for breakfast.

Chris Suddick

BITCHINESS IS THE BEST REVENGE

Angela Martin

Marian Henley

BITCHINESS IS THE BEST REVENGE
by Katherine McAlpine

Renounced, replaced, cast from your life,
I've become friends with your ex-wife
and cannot feel too glum or blue,
for we've had such fun trashing you.

MY BOYFRIEND AND I BROKE UP AND I'M GLAD I WAS A GIRL SCOUT.
by Flash Rosenberg

I learned to apply environmental conscientiousness to personal life.
It doesn't matter what I got out of the relationship.
The important thing is ... *He's doing great*.
He's healthier and better looking than when I met him.
He's more productive and creative.
And he has a beautiful, new, young girlfriend....

Good Scout that I am,
I left the campsite in better shape than I found it.

WELL, ANOTHER ONE BITES THE DUST! Funny how you can NOW see that you saw it coming only after it finally came..? Well, who NEEDS the bastard/bitch? You deserve MUCH better! And, to help clear the path, we present the...

GUARANTEED GET-OVER-IT KIT

(NON GENDER-EXCLUSIVE)

One month's supply of your favorite "consolation chow" in scientifically-measured quantities to prevent actual weight gain. COMING SOON: Low/zero-calorie versions so you can REALLY pork out!

LOTS of photos of gals/guys MUCH better-looking (and nicer) than ol' "what's-her/his-name"... Geared towards what you're recovering from / have sworn off forever/ are willing to consider NOW...

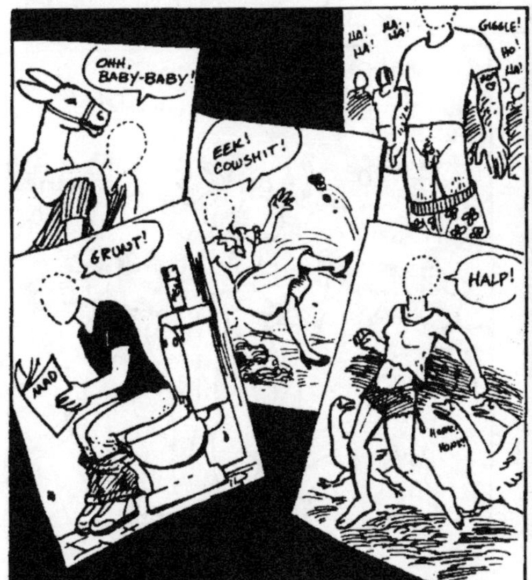

"Cut-up-old-photos-and-paste-on-their-face" pictures of people in silly, embarrassing and humiliating situations. This one REALLY works, folks!

Month's membership in the "get-it-off-your-chest" club. Special 800-number and Aunt Ethel's sympathetic ear for hours of blissful babbling. Lifetime package deal for those who seem to end up in the same sort of relationships time after time.

Chief! Look what just came in over the wires!
TICKA TICKA TICKA
tappity tap tappity
CITY DESK
Cece broke up with Gerald!
Great Scott!
Stop the presses!
VICTORY DAY!
Ta-ra ra BOOM deeay
That Gerald treated her like a DOORMAT!
MOBILE NEWS
HURRAY for Cece!
CECE IS FREE
Did you think she'd EVER ditch him?
No! We can hardly BELIEVE it!
Look! There she is!
WAHOO!
After all those years of taking his guff, how did you DO it, Cece?
Ta ra ra BOOM dee ay
Nerves of STEEL!
I... I don't KNOW
A will of IRON!
She's a fine example for women everywhere!
SNIFF
The entire WORLD is watching!
SPEECH! SPEECH!
So TELL it, sister!
I want him BACK...
cut the mike
©1986 Marian Henley

Alison Bechdel

UH-OH! LOCK UP YOUR INNER CHILDREN! IT'S CLEO BALDSHEIN, M.S.W. IN...

Guerilla Mediation

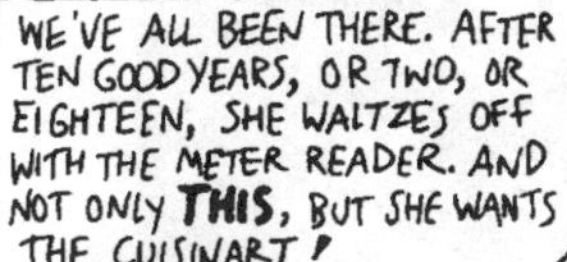

nina's adventures ©Nina Paley

I WORRY
by Wendy Cope

I worry about you—
So long since we spoke.
Love, are you downhearted,
Dispirited, broke?

I worry about you.
I can't sleep at night.
Are you sad? Are you lonely?
Or are you all right?

They say that men suffer,
As badly, as long.
I worry, I worry,
In case they are wrong.

THE CAT IS NOT IN THE MICROWAVE

Jennifer Berman

Today in Cat Obedience School, we'll be training our cats to use the scratching post!
DON'T you EVER EVER EVER even TOUCH this scratching post! Understand?!
That's why I bought this valuable antique couch...
So you could SCRATCH it, RIP it, and tear it to SHREDS!! See?
Scratch
Scritch
So please please please pretty PLEASE, tear up the antique couch!
Scratch
Scritch
Voila!
©1992 Marian Henley

THE CAT IS NOT IN THE MICROWAVE

by Sabrina Matthews

My mother was one of the first women in the United States to own a microwave, and she still won't leave it plugged in overnight. She has this fear that one of the cats will go into the kitchen, punch in a cook sequence, jump in, and pull the door shut behind itself, having first made a suicide pact with one of the other cats to hit the start button once it's in there. So every night before she goes to bed there is the locking of the house and the unplugging of the microwave.

When I visit my mother, I sleep downstairs on the couch because it gives the illusion that I can make a quick getaway. Mom will always want something from upstairs, and so in the middle of the night I'll hear, "Sabrina?" Maybe my mother is the only mother like this, like living in suspended animation, but the house has to be kept at a constant temperature of thirty-three and a quarter degrees. So I'm lying there with the quilt pulled all the way up to my neck, with my little fingers poking out and I'm reading a book. Everything's warm except my nose and my fingers. "Sabrina?"

"Yeah, Mom?"

"I haven't seen Grey in a while." My Mom's cats have really imaginative names. There's a grey one named Grey, a black one named Black, and a fat one named Big Teeny. So she calls down the stairs, "I haven't seen Grey in a while."

"Okay, Mom, you want me to go check the microwave?"

So I go in the kitchen, I check the microwave, because I can't lie to my mother, I'm freezing, but I check everything else that I can think of that a cat might fit, because I know what she's going to ask me. So I go back out, race onto the couch and get under the covers, nice and warm, and I call, "No, she's not in the microwave."

"Oh, thanks." Then I look at the watch. Thirty seconds on the dot: "Sabrina?"

"The cat is not in the freezer, the refrigerator, the dishwasher, the oven, the washing machine, or anywhere else that a cat can fit."

"Ok. Thanks."

Libby Reid

UNDERSTANDING YOUR KITTY CAT

Learn what she's trying to tell you the only way she knows how~by behaving in a way that makes you wish you were a mean person.

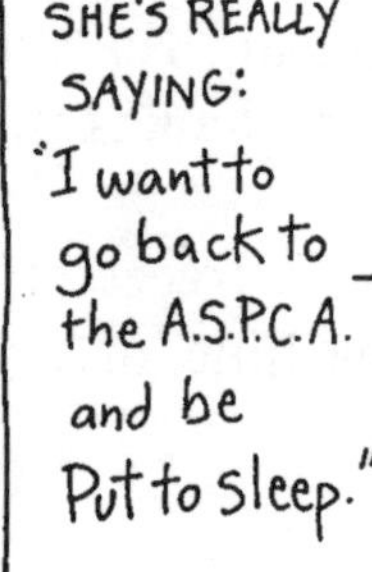

SUPER CATNIP
by Dorothy Heller

No catnip tree
Could offer bliss
Of magnitude
To equal this
As in a transport
Of delight
My spaced-out cougar
Spends the night
His nose in cosy
Rendezvous
With my malodorous
Jogging shoe.

Being alone never bothered her...

Stephanie Piro

Zrinka Jovicic

Jennifer Berman

Signe Wilkinson

Diane Germain

JANITOR AT FERTILIZATION LABORATORY IMPRISONED FOR MURDER AFTER HIS BROOM HANDLE KNOCKS 6 PETRI DISHES TO THE FLOOR KILLING ALL.

EVEN HARDENED POLICE VETERANS WERE SEEN WITH TEARS IN THEIR EYES AFTER WITNESSING THE TRAGIC CRIME SCENE WITH MAGNIFYING GLASSES. (SEE PAGE 7 FOR THE GRISLY DETAILS OF THE CARNAGE) HIS NEIGHBORS REACT WITH SHOCK AND DISBELIEF, " HE WAS SUCH A QUIET MAN "

Jennifer Camper

LET'S MAKE A DEAL

CAMPER © 89

OK, MEN CAN MAKE ABORTION LAWS...

...WHEN MERMAIDS START MAKING SHOES

I'M GETTING AN ABORTION

by Betsy Salkind

I'm getting an abortion. Well, I don't need one, but I feel that as an American I should exercise that right before it gets taken away.

And now that we have Judge Uncle Thomas, I mean Clarence, and David Souter on the Supreme Court, who by the way lives alone on a sheep farm in New Hampshire, I thought we needed some new legal strategies. One idea is to videotape our abortions. Then they would be protected under the First Amendment, as freedom of expression.

Or here's an idea that might appeal to Republicans. Fetal eviction. They don't pay rent, they're eating our food. It's a drain on the whole system. It's as bad as welfare.

I had a pro-choice party. I told people to come dressed as the person they most think should have been aborted. It was a disaster. This other woman came who was wearing the same dress I was wearing. We both came as the pope.

I don't really think the issue is abortion at all. I think the real issue is unwanted pregnancy. There's a lot of theories about why this happens. Some say it's a result of women's low self-esteem. I know that this is true, because last week I had low self-esteem one day...BAM pregnant, just like that.

So, I've been mailing all of my used tampons to the Supreme Court with little notes. Dear Justice Rhenquist. Since you're so concerned with my reproductive facilities, I've enclosed one of my eggs. Feel free to resuscitate and inseminate it. Love, Betsy.

Signe Wilkinson

CIVIL RIGHTS: A SHORT STORY

by Sheree Anne Bradford-Lea

I was sitting in a crowded bar, smoking section, waiting for my husband to show up and trying to dry off. The rain outside was torrential, and it seemed like the entire city had congregated here. I'd hoped someone would offer me a seat in the non-smoking section; maybe they just hadn't noticed a rotund pregnant woman shoving her way through the Friday afternoon crowd.

"Happy hour—what a misnomer!" I thought sourly. But at least now I could rest, dry, and relax. My husband and I were trying to make the most of getting out together now, knowing that after the baby was born it wouldn't be so easy. And this place served the best—and the most affordable—food in town. I started squeezing the hem of my shirt to get rid of excess water, thinking about what I'd order from the menu when my husband got here.

Suddenly I was attacked.

"What's she doing here?" a man drinking beer at the bar yelled, glaring at me. "Get out of here, lady."

"Why? What's wrong?" I asked, startled. I dropped my hem guiltily.

"You're pregnant," he shot back. "This is a bar. And it's the smoker's section. Get out!"

I sighed. It was just going to keep being one of those days, wasn't it? The rest of the patrons and the bartender had frozen waiting for my response. A thousand thoughts flashed through my head. But only two words came out of my mouth.

"Civil rights," I said.

"What?"

"You're trying to take away my civil rights!"

"It has nothing to do with civil rights! Joe, give me another beer!"

"Uh, I think you've had enough, Jack," the bartender said.

"It has everything to do with civil rights!" I snapped. "It's my freedom to choose!"

Jack slammed his beer glass onto the bar. "It'll endanger the baby!"

"The baby?" I asked. "What baby? Where? I don't see a baby."

"That one, right there, stupid broad," he said, pointing to my belly.

"You mean my fetus?" figuring the use of a clinical term would make him wince. It did. "You're talking about my fetus and you don't even know what to call it? And I'm supposed to listen to you? Get this straight, buddy, it's up to me to sift through information and decide what's safe for my fetus. Got that? It's mine, not yours." The man got red in the face.

"Come on, stop picking on her," the bartender said. "The woman has a right to sit wherever she likes."

But Jack's pal, sitting on the other side of him, came to his rescue. "Get out, lady," he hollered, banging his beer glass on the counter.

"Shut up, you damn drunk," someone else shouted.

The pal craned his neck around, squinting in the dim light. "You shut up," he yelled suddenly, lunging at the crowded table.

The brawl had begun.

"Maybe you'd better leave, lady," the bartender said softly as he dodged a flying bottle. "They might stop."

"But I'm not your problem," I protested, moving to another stool to avoid a couple of flying bodies, "They are. Do you really want to throw me out in the rain to appease that jerk?"

"Yeah, okay," the bartender said. He picked up the phone behind the bar. "If you don't knock it off I'm calling the cops!" he yelled to everyone.

In response a guy pulled the phone cord and snapped the jack out of the wall. The bartender grabbed him by the neck. "You're paying for that," he bellowed.

I was getting a little frightened. And angry. this certainly wasn't doing my "baby" any good. I decided it was fair to stop this brawl by any means I had at my disposal. And it was clear these bozos couldn't tell a woman who was seven months pregnant from one who was about to deliver.

"Ohhhh," I groaned loudly.

"What's the matter, lady?" the bartender leaned forward anxiously.

"Ohhhh!" I groaned, even louder. Sure enough, the fight had stopped.

"Uh oh," someone said.

"Now look what you've done," one man said to Jack.

"What I've done? Look, if she'd have left when I told her to—"

"Ohhhhhh!" I screamed.

"Do you want to lie down, lady?" the bartender asked. "Are you happy you ripped the phone out now?" he yelled at the guy who'd done it.

"A glass of water, please," I gasped. The water was brought and I quickly downed most of it. Then I sat up. "There, all better," I said.

They looked at me anxiously.

"That's it?" asked Jack.

"That's it," I said. "I guess it was just the stress of being yelled at, then all that fighting. I'm fine now."

"You should have left when I told you to."

"And gone where? Listen, you, maybe you should think about coming up with solutions, instead of just trying to tell people what to do."

"Yeah," someone from the crowd echoed.

For a moment I thought the whole thing was going to start over again, but Jack looked at my belly and thought better of it.

"I told her to get out," he muttered, going back to his seat.

"Idiot," I muttered back.

I watched the bartender busily taking the names of people who had caused damages and sipped my water. I could feel my baby moving inside me, gentle and rhythmic.

About ten minutes later my husband showed up.

"Sorry I'm late," he said, kissing me. He sat down and looked around at the overturned tables and smashed glass.

"Geez," he said, "What happened?"

"Nothing we couldn't handle," I replied, patting my belly. "It's not always easy to defend your civil rights. Especially in a bar."

Dianne Reum

Jennifer Berman

Young Dr. Jack Kevorkian Assisting Lemmings with Suicide.

Robin Watkins

...TELL ME IF THIS HURTS, MR. FLOYD.....NO? HOW ABOUT THIS... DOES THIS HURT...? NO?
HOW ABOUT THIS?
HOW ABOUT THIS?
TRY THIS! SEE IF THIS HURTS!
R. PICCOLO

TROTS and BONNIE

NEEDLING

by Wendy Lichtman

When the ophthalmologist said it was probably an allergy and the allergist said it was most likely a virus, I took my swollen, red, itching eyes to the acupuncturist. She put her hand on my wrist, felt my pulse, and said it was certainly my liver.

Oh, come off it.

Before my first appointment for acupuncture, I had received a very detailed questionnaire that took about forty minutes to fill out at home. The main thing I was struck with was that the several-page-long form seemed so personal.

I was used to those one-page things western doctors give you on a clipboard in their waiting rooms. Those forms that ask the dates of my immunizations, if my maternal grandmother had diabetes and, most importantly, the name and number of my insurance carrier.

But Dr. Magin's questionnaire asked things like, "Do you move your bowels when you travel?" Imagine. Well, it so happens that I don't, and I always presumed this was a unique, and slightly crazy, problem of mine. Sure, if I'm out of town for a month, I'll poop in a strange toilet, but for only a weekend away, it's not likely.

Now, I can't tell you how much the asking of that question meant to me. It meant, if it was on the questionnaire, that other people must also be plagued during their travels by psychosomatic constipation. It meant that I was not alone. I don't know if I can explain how much this delighted me.

Okay, picture one of your personal idiosyncrasies, one that you have never discussed with anyone, because you know it's nuts, and you know that only you do it. Say, for example, you turn off your car radio whenever you drive over the Bay Bridge because you want to be sure you hear the earthquake if it happens when you're suspended in the air between San Francisco and Oakland. Well, there you are filling out a questionnaire for a health care provider and it asks the question, "Do you turn off your car radio when you are on the Bay Bridge?" It doesn't matter what you answer—you are so delighted at being *asked* the question, because it must mean you are not psychotic.

That's how Kinsey got all his fabulous information about sex. He asked questions that made people feel they were not alone in their behavior. Sure, other researchers had tried to figure out if anyone, other than themselves, masturbated. But what they asked the people who answered their doors was "Do you masturbate?"

No, no, no, they replied. Of course not.

Kinsey simply rephrased it. "How often do you masturbate?" he asked, and people were so thrilled to be validated about a behavior that they had never before discussed, that they answered daily, weekly, monthly or never.

So there I was in nosy Dr. Magin's office. My eyes were hurting, and nearly puffed closed. "Well," said the doctor, when she gently put her hand on my wrist and pressed firmly, "you certainly are putting out a lot more energy than you are getting in." This from feeling my pulse?

But for some reason, I guess because it was true, when she said this, I started to cry, and she pushed different points on my back and chest with her small strong fingers to get the energy that was stuck flowing, and all the time I'm still thinking, Oh, come off it.

The needles are hair-thin, and Dr. Magin pops them in with a tap of her finger, and I look like the guy in Ripley's who is hammering nails up his nose to get a little attention. But they don't hurt, and I can't imagine why. Except for one. When she inserted the one right above my big toe, I yelled and sat up to see what she had done.

"I was afraid you'd feel that one," Dr. Magin

said sympathetically. "It's the eyes."

Oh, come off it.

"Would you like to see the chart?" she asked, in a gently clinical tone.

"I don't want to see any chart," I grumbled, lying back down. "This is all voodoo, but I like you."

"I like you too," she said, popping a needle into my neck.

After the third session, my eyes, which had been irritating me for three months, were normal. But I continued coming for treatment, because we had found a lot of other things that weren't. Mostly, I was uncomfortable because of nightly hot flashes and other hormonally related problems. For nearly a year I had been waking up sweaty, unable to get consistent sleep at night.

She prescribed me herbs with Chinese names and pretty little sketches of flowers on the labels. With a straight face she told me to take two, three times a day before meals.

I was taking my herbs and getting my needles for about six weeks, when I was put in the office with four colorful lithographs. Naked but for my little hospital gown, I had been admiring the prints while I waited for the doctor. As I got off the examining table to see one better, the artist's biography caught my eye. The artist, pictured in a smock, a large one, holding a paintbrush in her trunk, was an Asian elephant named Ruby from the Phoenix zoo.

"Marvelous, aren't they?" Dr. Magin asked, bustling in with my chart, all medical-looking, not appearing at all to be the insane woman she obviously is. "Ruby was a very disturbed elephant," she reported sadly, "until she started to paint for therapy." For therapy, yet.

As I climbed onto the examining table, backwards, so as not to look too much like Ruby in her smock, the doctor said happily, "I'm so grateful I could acquire these. I'm hoping I can get one more, if it's available, but now they are terribly expensive, of course."

Of course. I allowed this person to stick needles in very tender places and talk therapeutically to me.

When I appeared for my eighth session, I reported to the doctor that something strange was going on in my body. I had not, in about two months, awakened in the middle of the night sweaty.

Dr. Magin stopped writing in my chart. She looked pleased. As always, she picked up my wrist before she began treatment. "Ah, yes," she said, with satisfaction.

"I have no idea why," I told her.

Still holding my wrist, smiling, Dr. Magin didn't say anything. But I suspect, actually, I'm nearly positive, she wanted to say, Oh, come off it.

Confused? Now's the time to Ask Aunt Violet

Q: I'm worried. My lover and I have no medical insurance. We are getting older, and we have a very modest income. We may even want to start a family. The Clintons don't seem to be moving fast enough—we *can't* wait 'til *1997* to go to the doctor. What to do? —Queen-For-a-Year, At Least

A: YES, I *KNOW* THE SITUATION IS *DIRE* RIGHT NOW. BUT THERE *MAY* BE *HOPE*. I FOUND THE FOLLOWING FLYER ON MY WINDSHIELD. HOPEFULLY, IT'LL BE *JUST THE THING* YOU NEED. GOOD LUCK!

Join the MEDICAL INSURANCE of the MONTH™ CLUB

JUST DIAL 1-800-COVER ME.!!

Are you tired, rundown...and without Medical Insurance? Join the other 2 or 3 Proud Americans who belong to the Medical Insurance of the Month™ Club. With MIM™ Club, you can pick 'n' choose from our economical 4-month plan or luxuriate in our Super Deluxe 12-month coverage.

And all for ONLY $9.99 a month!

(Prices slightly higher in Marin & Westchester counties; Hawaii; and Nantucket in the summer.)

February

is Cancer month! Yup, if you're gonna get The Big C, why not do it in February? Who wants depressing, nauseating treatments in a long, hot month like July? Get Cancer in February and get it over with.

May

May is Baby Month on the versatile MIMC Plan, and May 24th is SPECIAL BONUS BABY DAY. Any baby born on May 24th, you get free! So go ahead, HAVE that little bundle of joy in May—and save your*self* a bundle!

August

Fog getting you down? August is Psychiatry Month. Therapy sessions subject to availability.

October

Why not get a Sex Change operation this October? By Halloween you'll be out partying, while all your friends will still be home primping.

C'MON, GIRLS LET'S PARTY!

JANUARY....Organ Transplant Jamboree
MARCH....Dermatology
APRIL....Sports Injuries/Orthopedics
JUNE....Scarification/Tattoo Removal
JULY....Gastroenterology Gala
SEPTEMBER....Festival of Dental Health
NOVEMBER....Genital Maintenance
DECEMBER....Plastic Surgery for Tots

Alternative Health Care Month

We now offer a special floating Alternative Health Care Month™ as an option. Reproduce cheaply & naturally with our popular home SQUAT'n'TOT™ birth-it-yourself kit; Change your appearance holistically with a Homeoplastic™ Remedy; or choose a *painless* Acupuncture Circumcision for your child.

Car Accident? Have it in April. THIS COUPON ENTITLES BEARER TO ONE (1) *EMERGENCY ROOM VISIT* in *APRIL*.

THIS COUPON ENTITLES BEARER TO AN UNLIMITED NUMBER OF RUDE MEDICAL RECEPTIONISTS *all year long!*

Send your most heartstring-tugging questions to Aunt Violet, SF Weekly, 425 Brannan St. SF 94107 © 1-25-93 Caryn Leschen

Anxious Moments in dreamland

Forgot to check the brakes

Forgot to attend math class all semester

Forgot to wear shirt and shoes to work

Forgot how to run

Bonnie Timmons

DREAMS

by Lorrie Sprecher

Today at work we were talking about stupid professors, and my friend said she once took a psychology class in college all about dreams. She was under a lot of stress at the time and dreamed that she was falling.

When she asked about it, the white professor said, "Of course you dreamed that. It's a black dream. All black people have dreams that they're falling."

"All black people?" she said. "Let me get this right. It has nothing to do with stress? It has to do with black, and all black people, all over the world, no matter who they are or how they live, dream the same?"

He said, "All black people have unhappy dreams that they're falling."

She told me, "I asked him to show it to me, but he couldn't find it written down anywhere."

I said, "All last night I dreamed that I was falling."

She said, "Then you must be black."

"Sister," I said, "I have to tell my parents."

"No wonder you're so edgy, you've been living all this time in somebody else's skin."

She and I had been born in the same hospital in Prince George's County, Maryland. And in 1960 it was segregated so they wouldn't let us be born on the same side.

"Look what they did to you," she said, "it's a shame. They put you in an incubator and turned out the light."

One of our white coworkers walked up, heard us talking dreams again, and said, "Last night I dreamed I gave birth to a squirrel."

"That's a white dream," I said. "All white people dream they're giving birth to a squirrel."

My shrink says birth is so traumatic it's lucky infants don't remember it or they wouldn't live. I think life is traumatic, being put with all those white babies, and losing a whole identity just like that.

When I told her about it, my shrink said, "Are either of your parents black?"

And I said, "What's that got to do with me?"

Nicole Hollander

THE WORLD OF HER DREAMS

Shary Flenniken

Chris Suddick

DOGS DOING THEIR BUSINESS ON THE NEIGHBORS' LAWN

Jennifer Berman

Lee Binswanger

DOGGED DUO
by Joyce La Mers

Each day at dawn
   I'm off to jog,
The leash I'm on
   Held by my dog.

Nicole Ferentz

FAX TERRIER
by Flash Rosenberg

I'm not getting a FAX machine
until I can get a FAX terrier.
I need a dog stationed,
READY to immediately EAT
those faxes so urgently sent.
It's only fair.
As communication technology advances,
it's essential to have ever more evolved excuses.

TROTS AND BONNIE
PEPSI... I THINK YOUR DOG MAY BE SICK.
NO, HE'S NOT.
HE'S DEAD.
...AND FREEZE-DRIED.
IT'S A NEW TECHNIQUE FOR PRESERVING OUR RELATIONSHIPS WITH OUR BELOVED ANIMAL PALS AFTER THEY PASS ON TO THAT GREAT KENNEL IN THE SKY.
OF COURSE, I NEVER ACTUALLY KNEW SPARKY WHEN HE WAS ALIVE.... HE'S A PRE-OWNED PET. HIS ORIGINAL FAMILY COULDN'T KEEP HIM BECAUSE HE WAS SCARING THE NEW PUPPY.
HE'S MUCH MORE VERSATILE THAN A LIVE PET.
CAN YOU DO THIS?
HE IS HARD TO WALK, THOUGH.... MAYBE I SHOULD INSTALL WHEELS.
YOU SHOULD TRY IT WITH TROTS.
WHAT A GOOD IDEA... OF COURSE, HE'D ALSO MAKE A NICE RUG.
THAT'S CHESTER...
HIS OWNER WAS RUN OVER BY A CAR.
MAYBE I'LL JUST FREEZE-DRY MY FAVORITE HOUSEPLANTS INSTEAD.
I THINK I'VE LOST MY TASTE FOR FREEZE-DRIED COFFEE.

Shary Flenniken

It's simple, Cece! Men are ANIMALS...
...and there's nothing wrong with that!
EVERYTHING is wrong with that! It's an offensive, dated STEREOTYPE!
Alright, men! Speak up for your-selves! Tell her like it is! SAY SOMETHING! SPEAK! SPEAK!
How can you be so unfair? Men aren't ANIMALS! They're HUMAN BEINGS!
You can't convince me!
ARF!
See? He said...
What did he say?
WOOF!
No, I think he said "ARF"
©1996 Marian Henley

Jennifer Berman

Jennifer Berman

QUOTE REPAIR

by Flash Rosenberg

I've always loved quotes. Quotes concisely package thoughts so much neater than it ever feels just mumbling through the gabby confusion of life. Not religion, but a well-turned phrase is the only thing (well, okay, besides sex or food) that gives me some brief sense of Universal Truth. But over time, many old proverbs have grown a bit shabby. Out-of-touch. Their wit has wilted. But with a little heckling and tweaking, the following standard platitudes have been repaired by playing "Quote Doctor."

The lovers of freedom will be free.—Burke
quote repair: *The freedom of lovers will be expensive.*

Sloth makes all things difficult.—Franklin
quote repair: *It is difficult to make a sloth.*

It is better to bend than to break.—French Proverb
quote repair: *It is better to take a break.*

Idleness is the holiday of fools.—Chesterfield
quote repair: *Holidays fool us into idleness.*

Wit is the salt of conversation, not the food.—Hazlitt
quote repair: *Food causes witless conversation about salt.*

The cautious seldom err.—Confucius
quote repair: *The erroneous are seldom caught.*

continued...

A delay is better than a disaster.
quote repair: *It's no disaster to get laid.*

Innocence is ashamed of nothing.—Rousseau
quote repair: add *...except its innocence.*

Catch the bear before you sell his skin.
quote repair: *You'll catch hell if you bare your skin.*

The echo always has the last word.—German Proverb
quote repair: add *...except in that sentence where "word" is the last word.*

A friend is someone before whom I may think aloud.—Ralph Waldo Emerson
quote repair: *Before someone is allowed to be my friend I have to think.*

Nothing is so easy as to deceive one's self.
—Demosthenes
quote repair: *Nothing is so deceptive as to see yourself as easy.*

Too much scruple is only concealed pride.
—Goethe
quote repair: *Too much pride is only congealed scrapple.*

All work and no play makes Jack a dull boy.
—English Proverb
quote repair: *Dull work and no boys makes one jack-off.*

Forbidden things have a secret charm.—Tacitus
quote repair: *Secreting things are forbidden to be charming.*

Men learn while they teach.—Seneca
quote repair: add *...which means that men teach what they haven't learned.*

Study the past if you want to divine the future.
—Confucius
quote repair: *Study the divan if you want to patch furniture.*

Friendship is the band of reason.—Sheridan
quote repair: *Reasonable friends don't start a band.*

If you keep saying things are going to be bad, you have a good chance of being a prophet.—Isaac Bashevis Singer
quote repair: *If you keep saying you need a profit, you have a good chance of doing bad things.*

We are less convinced by what we hear than what we see.—Euripides
quote repair: add *...and we see even less when we're already convinced.*

True enjoyment cannot be described.—Rousseau
quote repair: add *...unless what you enjoy is the failed attempt to describe true enjoyment.*

I am nothing, but truth is everything.—Lincoln
quote repair: *I am everything and everything is nothing; And I am nothing and I am you and you are me; And we are all together within you and without you; I am the walrus goo goo ga choob…*

The gift of a bad man can bring no good.
—Euripides
quote repair: *Bring me the gift of a good man to make me bad.*

They conquer who believe they can.—Virgil
quote repair: add *...get away with it.*

Grief is a tree that has only tears for fruit.
—Philemon
quote repair: *The grief of fruit is to be torn from a tree.*

He that asketh faintly beggeth a denial.—Fuller
quote repair: *He that speaketh with so much "eth" is beggeth-ed by everyone to shut up.*

The journey of 1000 miles begins with one step. —Lao-Tze
quote repair: add ...*and the singing of 1000 bottles of beer on the wall.*

Better an empty purse than an empty head. —German Proverb
quote repair: add ...*but an empty bed is going too far.*

One cannot always be a hero, but one can always be a man.—Goethe
quote repair: add ...*unless you're a woman... in which case you cannot even be included in a quote from another century.*

No pleasure lasts long unless there's some variety in it.—Syrus
quote repair: *No society lasts long unless there's some pleasure in it.*

Not many men have both good fortune and good sense.—Livy
quote repair: *It is good fortune to have many men, but it doesn't make good sense.*

Every why hath a wherefore.—Shakespeare
quote repair: Basic fill *"anything in the blank" mode*:

> *Every ________hath a________.*
> *Every where hath a what?*
> *Every Y hath a foyer.*
> *Every whore hath a cry.*
> *Every hath hath a hat with an H.*
> *Every who hath a what-for?*
> *Every Horton hatches a hoo.—Dr. Seuss*

No duty is more urgent than that of returning thanks.—St. Ambrose
quote repair: *No urge is more dirty than that of regurgitating drinks.*

Happy are those who have no doubt of themselves.—Flaubert
quote repair: *Stupid are those who have no doubt of themselves.*

IN PRAISE OF BEST GIRLFRIENDS

Jessica Bruce

Trina Robbins

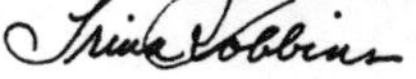

Marian Henley

IN PRAISE OF BEST GIRLFRIENDS

by Stephanie Brush

They don't give college courses in How to Be a Best Friend. They don't teach courses in How to Find One, either. There's no "Friendz 'R' Us" Personalized Dating Services you can sign up for. If you're lucky, you stumble upon a lifelong Best Friend by accident.

Like walking into a telephone pole. A nice telephone pole. It's a lot harder than finding a husband, I've discovered, and only a million times more important.

A year ago, I would not have said this, but it's Thanksgiving and gratitude is in the air. (Thanksgiving is a day of Compulsory Gratitude, which is a good thing. Like scheduling kissing in a busy relationship—it's better to mark it on the calendar than not observe it at all.)

I have got a lot of female friends in this life, and most of them have turned out to be, I've recently discovered, Acting Best Friends—in much the way that Dan Quayle is supposedly president of the Senate. (There isn't exactly a vacuum of power, in other words, but you just don't feel quite ... well, you know what I mean.)

There has to be extraordinary chemistry in a friendship, is what I think I'm saying. And by this, I mean: Mouth Chemistry. MOTORmouth chemistry. Otherwise, all you have is a fond acquaintanceship.

No man will ever understand this, but the main prerequisites for friendship are 1) nonstop talking-at-the-same-time for at *least* 7 1/2 hours, followed by 2) going home and then calling each other up on the phone in order to discuss all the things which were not discussed in person. In the case of my best friend, Judith, it is particularly hopeless, because she is a columnist, like me. We 1) see each other in person, then we 2) call each other immediately on the phone, then we 3) write each other letters about the things that weren't discussed in person, then we 4) send each other copies of the column we wrote about the visit and the phone call.

How did I decide that Judith was going to be my friend? This was easy.

When I first visited her at her house, I saw immediately that she had the same Purina Cat Chow ad taped to her refrigerator. This struck me as not only cosmic but decisive.

Also, her husband is not a jerk. It's amazing how many Best Friends insist on acquiring wholly unacceptable husbands. If Best Friends were required to fill out a form before acquiring a husband, the world would be a better place, but so few of them show this kind of courtesy.

So now, let's review the criteria so far: 1) Nonstop talking, 2) Identical refrigerator art, 3) Acceptable (or at least non-jerk) husband. Some would say: Who could ask for more?

But I have omitted the most important trait of all: Generosity.

By this, I do not mean "free with money". Very few women care about that type of stuff. Money was invented by men, and then men invented office buildings so that they could have a place to talk about their money and write amounts of money on pieces of paper and fax them to each other.

When I say "generosity", I think that any woman will know what I mean. I mean a generosity of spirit: a lack of pettiness, and lack of jealousy, and a meeting (or close to it) of the minds. "This is obvious," you say, but alas, it is hard to find in a friend.

I had a Best Friend for a while who was a professional therapist. A very nice woman, actually. Unfortunately, therapists and humor columnists do not get along very well.

The first time I saw the therapist's house, I

said, "Oh, wow! This house is a dump!" (It was a gorgeous house, and everyone knew it and said so.) But "Marion" looked at me and said, "Stephanie. You seem a little hostile."

"It was a joke!" I said. Marion looked at me as if I had a frog crawling out of my eye.

"Marion" and I tried to be friends for a while, but we had radically different philosophies of life. Her philosophy was that I was out of my mind; my philosophy was also that I was out of my mind but that I deserved to be paid for it.

After a while I stopped seeing "Marion" because I felt she was excessively biased in favor of rational, tasteful behavior.

Luckily, my friend Judith agrees with this wholeheartedly.

To wit, I recently called Judith up and said, "What's your Thanksgiving column about?"

"It's about liposuction," she said. "It's about how every time I look at jellied cranberry sauce, I think that it must be the stuff that they go and vacuum..."

"That's disgusting," I said. "Can I steal that idea?"

"Sure," she said.

But the thing is, you see, I lied to my best friend; my column is not about jellied cranberry sauce—it is about her.

And now I have to pencil 7 1/2 hours into my schedule so that we can talk about it. The screaming alone should take 4 1/2. I am not sure whose dump we will meet in.

Nina Paley

Anne Gibbons

Viv Quillin

ODE TO A SHOPPING MALL

by Cyn Zarco

They wear the clothes they buy here
to buy the clothes they wear.

Stephanie Piro

Betsey Johnson made her feel
like a woman...
She wished she could say the
same for Kyle...

LOOKING FOR DUDS AT THE NEW
SHOP
WOW-A NEW BOUTIQUE!
©Lee Binswanger
I GUESS IT'S WORTH A LOOK.
NO...NO...NO, UGLY COLOR,...OH, NICE! MY SIZE, TOO.
FIFTY BUCKS FOR A PAIR OF COTTON PANTS!!
OH, MISS! CLERK!
TOO RICH FOR MY TASTE...
YEEKS! $ $ $
CLERK, I NEED YOUR OPINION.
DAZZLE
WHICH LOOKS BETTER?
THE SILVER OR THE GOLD LAMÉ?
SHIMMER
LEMME OUT OF THIS HIGH-PRICED JUNGLE TOOT SWEET!
WANT MY OPINION? WITH THE GOLD, YOU LOOK LIKE A HOOKER AND WITH THE SILVER, YOU LOOK LIKE A FLOOZY!
SPARKLE
OK, I'LL GO WITH THE SILVER!

Deb Donnelley

First Waltz

DRESSING FOR THE OCCASION

by Brenda Lawlor

It took a lot of self-discipline to drag myself away from my air-conditioned house, but I finally attacked the jungle in my backyard last Saturday morning. The corner of my yard next to the woods had grown into a thicket of honeysuckle vines and blackberry bushes. I armed myself with my son's machete and started to work.

I was just getting my momentum into high gear when Betsy stopped by. Betsy is a dear friend, but she never understands my eccentricities and invariably demands an explanation of my unorthodox methods.

"Why are you wearing a three-piece linen suit and high heels with stockings to do your yard work? Why is your briefcase leaned against that scrub oak tree?"

"I'm afraid of snakes," I answered.

Betsy looked puzzled. The woman is a great accountant, but she is completely devoid of imagination and creativity. I knew I'd have to give her a complete explanation.

"Okay, Betsy. Picture the scenario. I'm out here in the middle of my minijungle and nick a snake with my machete. What happens next?"

Betsy was beginning to get the big picture. "The snake would bite you, of course, and then you'd scream and I'd faint. Your nosy neighbor who's peeking out the window would probably think I'd had cardiac arrest and call an ambulance to take us to the emergency room."

"Now Betsy, let me ask you a personal question. Have you ever been to the emergency room when you were neatly dressed, had your makeup on and had your insurance forms neatly organized in your briefcase?"

"Heavens, no! Everybody knows you only end up in the emergency room when you look like a thrift shop reject."

"That's exactly my point. As long as I do my yard work in my Sunday clothes and have my insurance papers ready, I don't have to fear snake bites, black widow spider bites or even cutting my finger on this rusty machete."

Betsy's face lit up with understanding. "Let me run home and change clothes and pick up my briefcase. I'll put on my new designer dress and be right back to help you."

Nicole Hollander

Kathryn LeMieux

STRESSED FOR SUCCESS!

Debby Earthdaughter

bulbul

... LIKE MY LATEST OUTFIT?

Stephanie Piro

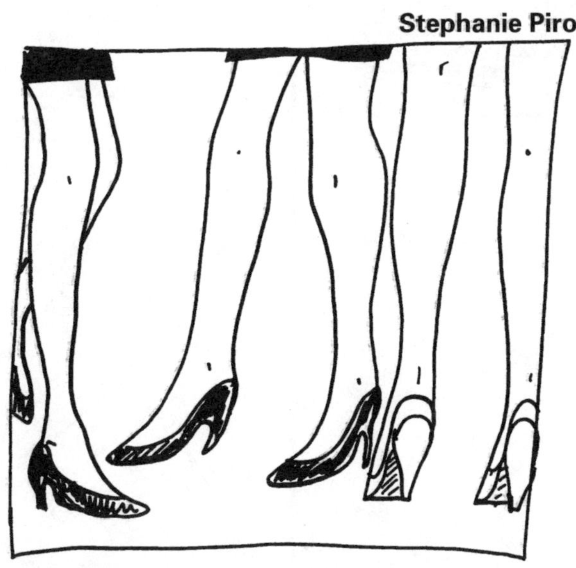

They hurt and they made your feet sweat... why did men find that so attractive?

Rina Piccolo

Andrea Natalie

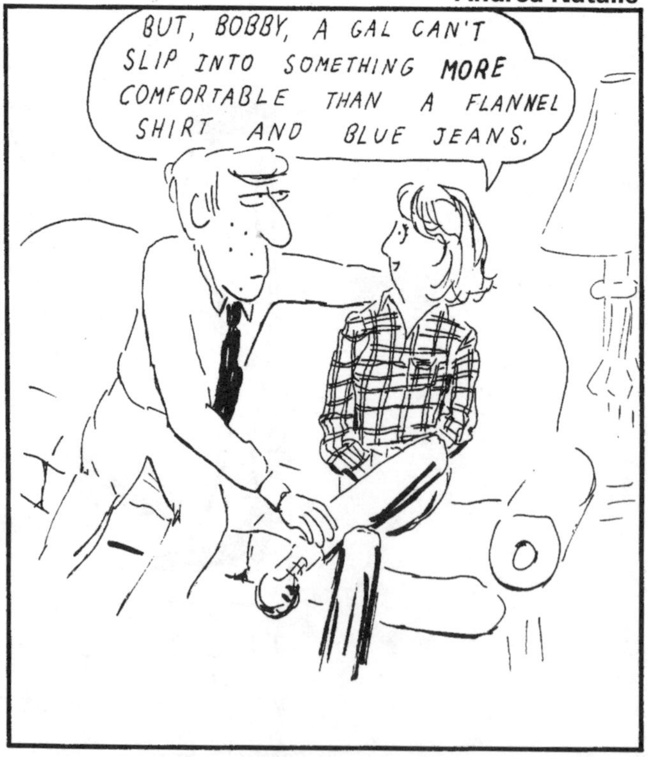

BUT, BOBBY, A GAL CAN'T SLIP INTO SOMETHING **MORE** COMFORTABLE THAN A FLANNEL SHIRT AND BLUE JEANS.

Early signs of lesbianism

Barbara Brandon

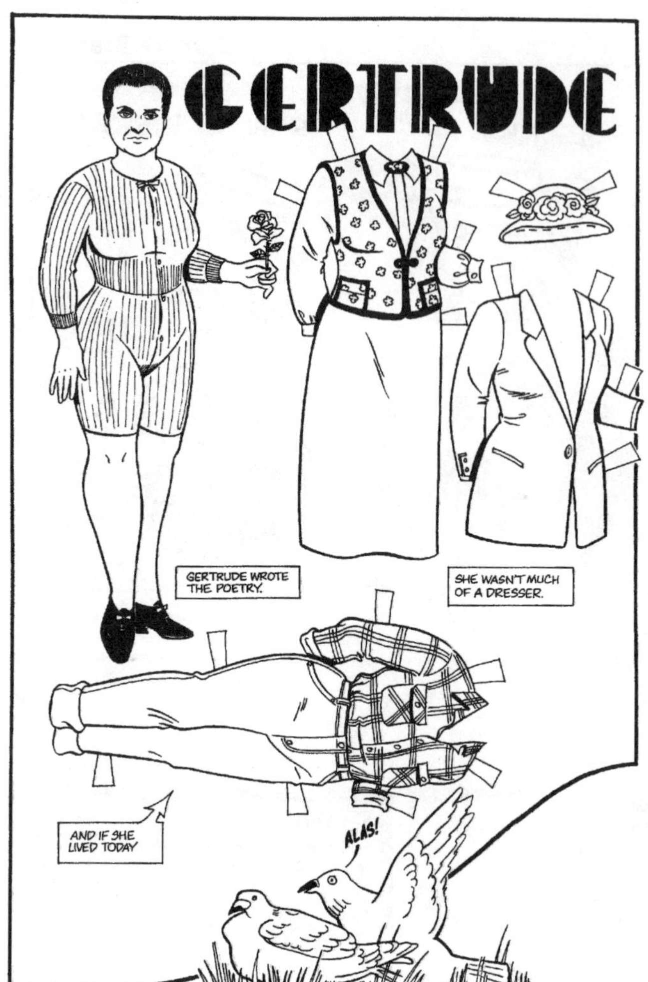

Trina Robbins

HOME IMPROVEMENTS

Constance Houck

NOTHING'S AN ACCIDENT IN INTERIOR DESIGN

by Adair Lara

I have begun to think I should do something with my place. It's a rental, and all we did is move in, set everything down and start arguing about TV programs. I'd like to fix it up a little, so the kids and I can entertain our friends—on purpose, for a change, instead of when we don't know we're doing it.

I don't know the first thing about interior design, and neither do the kids—at least I didn't think we did. Lately I've been leafing through house magazines for ideas, and I'm pleased to learn we have an unconscious flair for this sort of thing.

For example, the editor of *French Vogue*, like me, never redoes an apartment. "It is more challenging," she informs us, "to impose my taste within a set of limitations."

So true. Although my own limitations—lack of money, lack of time, lack of taste, lack of interest—are probably more challenging than hers, I think the kids and I have managed to impose our taste on the place despite them.

Patrick's room, for example, illuminates Herbert Muschamp's meaning when he said in *HG*, "We want a place for everything, but not necessarily everything in its place."

Nothing is in its place in Patrick's room. The shoes spilling sand on the bed, the quilt flowing to the linoleum, the cereal dish in the sock drawer—all sum up the relaxed aesthetic of the on-the-go 9-year-old.

In his sister Morgan's room the look is even more unspoiled—the bed unmade, all the drawers pulled out and clothes, some of them looking suspiciously like mine, flooding the floor and eddying over the lamps and bookshelves. This is clothing used as art, a leading trend in house magazines. Morgan, reclining on a pile of laundry, is taking it even one stop further—clothing used as furniture.

It's uncanny. One designer might almost have had the three bikes blocking our hallway in mind when he described his own deliberately cramped apartment. "The space is impossible to walk casually through," he said. "You take notice of things when you must step aside, walk cautiously and glance back."

I eagerly read on. In another magazine, a designer invites visitors to observe how, in his dazzling million-dollar apartment, "found, discarded and mundane things share weight and importance with art objects."

This is welcome news. The found, the mundane and the discarded account for such a substantial part of my furnishings that they have crowded out the art objects altogether. This doesn't matter. It's clear from my reading that you don't need art, or even taste, if you make a bold enough statement.

After all it was in the *HG*, again, that an essayist quoted Baudelaire. "What is intoxicating about bad taste," he said, "is the aristocratic pleasure of not pleasing."

This pleasure can be had in every corner of our apartment, from the sinking mauve couch in the living room to the upended picnic cooler serving as a fourth chair in the kitchen. The cooler doesn't belong there, which means it breaks aesthetic ground, as does the car fender one designer keeps in his living room.

People in design magazines leave a lot of stuff on the floor—paintings, pre-Columbian urns, Christmas lights flung in corners in July. This is to "draw the eye downward." We've been doing this for years, using mainly skateboards and Lego parts, but sometimes adding jackets, Popsicle wrappers and fallen Christmas ornaments, depending on the season.

In the end, I put the house magazines away. There seems to be nothing we can learn from them.

HOW TO OUT-TIDY A TIDEYBOLE

by Liz Scott

There are two kinds of neighbors you can have. The kind with junk cars all over their lawn and window screens pushed out and stuff dangling from the rafters that you don't even want to ask what it is. These are the good kind.

And then there's the kind with a lawn that looks like it has been cut with a manicure scissors and the front door polished and the curtains at the windows white as the driven snow. They are the bad kind.

I got a set of each, one on each side of me. The first set I call the Scumms. They got three pet dogs, two pet cats, and a bunch of mice that ain't pets. They also got kids—about as many as they got mice. And they either got a pig or one of the kids is pretty funny-looking.

The ones on the other side are the Tideyboles: Lysolla and her husband Nerd and their ten-year-old daughter Pristine. You know the type—Lysolla starches her bras to make them iron better; Nerd goes to the park to wash his car so he don't get the driveway damp; Pristine puts on an apron to eat a Popsicle—that kind of stuff.

The Scumms are good neighbors because no matter how terrible our house looks, theirs is worse. I get my Christmas decorations down by Mardi Gras at least, but they put Christmas lights up five years ago and they're still up. The grandmother plugs them in every night, thinking it is the TV. Then she complains the set is broken and goes to bed, so they don't tell her nothing. But they don't turn off the lights neither. You see them in August, twinkling around the masking tape on the windows that probably dates back twenty-one years to Hurricane Camille. Sometimes I can spend a whole day staring over at their house and mine seems cleaner by the minute without me ever picking up a thing.

But looking at the Tideyboles' house is as depressing as looking at a *Playboy* centerfold. Because I know that no matter how hard I work at it, what I got ain't ever going to look that good.

I got kids who got the Midas touch in dirt. Anything they pick up, they stain. I got a husband who thinks the best way to eat dry cereal is to sprawl out in front of the TV, open the box, and chug-a-lug it like beer. I got a survival sofa. If we was stranded with nothing but the sofa, we could stay alive for a week just on what's in it. Anything you need to sustain a human life you can find somewhere under them cushions.

But even if I got my house cleaned up for the Pope, it still wouldn't look as good as the Tideyboles' looks when the Orkin man walks in.

For one thing, Pristine has learned how to sleep in a bed without messing it up. She showed Gargoyle how she does this. She just sort of squats on the pillow, oozes under the covers, don't move a muscle for eight hours, and then oozes out again in the morning. And the bed still looks made. After Gargoyle has slept in a bed, it looks like there was one of them mud-wrestling matches in it.

Maybe I could take all this better if Lysolla didn't always have to be telling me about all her little routines that keep her house so nice. On Wednesday, she shines the tub with Jubilee kitchen wax. On Thursday, she turns the mattresses and sprays them with mattress freshener. Friday is wax-the-garage-floor day.

Only one time—one time—did I ever get one up on her. I will always remember that day. It is Sunday, the toilet won't flush, and Gargoyle is missing his little robot-that-turns-into-a-baby-machine-gun, which he left on the back of the seat. We only got one toilet, so this is an emergency that is getting worse by the minute. We try with the plumber's friend and we try with a hanger, but we can't get it unstuck.

Finally Lout unbolts the whole thing and drags it outside and I get out the garden hose. So there I am in the front yard, holding a hose in the toilet, waiting for a robot or a machine gun to wash out. And along comes Lysolla, just getting home from church with Nerd and Pristine in tow. Of course, she asks what in the world I am doing.

I guess I got a mean streak I didn't know about, or I guess the devil makes me do it. What I do, I raise my eyebrows, and I say, "What do you mean, what am I doing? Don't *you* deep-clean your toilet every Sunday?"

And I watch her go in her house and I hear her yell for her husband. I knew Nerd is going to be busy with the pipe wrench in a minute. And for once, looking at her house, I feel good.

WORLD LITERATURE: WHAT'S THE POINT?

EMILY DICKINSON
by Wendy Cope

Higgledy-piggledy
Emily Dickinson
Liked to use dashes
Instead of full stops.

Nowadays, faced with such
Idiosyncrasy,
Critics and editors
Send for the cops.

Catherine Goggia

MUSIC APPRECIATION

by Lynda Barry

Well, one thing that they never tell you in grade school is to enjoy singing while you can because eventually you are going to be divided up by who can sing and who can't sing, and the people who can sing will go to Choir, and the ones who can't sing won't sing, and may never sing again, and go to the class called "Music Appreciation" where a teacher will give you a piece of cardboard printed with the life-size keys of a piano and then teach you how to play "Go Tell Aunt Rhody" on it to a record.

How you get tested for your singing is, the first week of junior high school you report to the auditorium during music period and find out you have to stand alone on the stage except for a ninth grader playing the piano, and sing "America the Beautiful" while the rest of the class sits around drawing on their folders or staring at you while they wait for their turns. You get a score and then that's it. The End.

If you are too scared to sing by yourself, you can forfeit, but you automatically go to Music Appreciation. It's a big school and they don't have time to fool around.

Rina Piccolo

WORLD LITERATURE: WHAT'S THE POINT?

by Candyce Meherani

You remember Literature: Books written by dead people for the purpose of teaching you Important Life Lessons. But did you remember the Important Life Lessons, or did you go out and screw up your life as if Herman Melville hadn't given himself a bad case of writer's cramp trying to teach you a thing or two? Let's find out:

1. *Moby Dick* is:
   a. A cautionary tale about everything that can go wrong on a cruise ship.
   b. A complex moral tale with homoerotic undercurrents in which the whale is thought to represent Nature, Fate and/or Reality.
   c. One of the greatest hard-core porn flicks ever mentioned in a Senate hearing.

2. *Paradise Lost* is:
   a. The pop psych term for that sick feeling you get the first time you realize your new marriage partner isn't any better than the old one.
   b. An epic poem that grapples with the deepest questions of human existence—creation, evil, redemption.
   c. A hot new L.A. dance club.

3. *Robin Hood's Adventures* is:
   a. A TV docudrama about a classic kleptomaniac with peripheral chronic conduct disorder.
   b. A group of folktales that celebrate the virtues of courage, righteous revenge, good aim, leadership, brotherhood and social welfare.
   c. A group of folktales that have often been attacked by roving bands of Hollywood moguls.

4. *The Prince* is:
   a. The wonderful man you're always waiting for, but who will not come until you spend many, many hours in therapy discussing what it is about you that's keeping him away.
   b. A ruthless instruction manual for getting and keeping power over other people, written by Niccolo Machiavelli in the 1500s.
   c. A small African-American musician from the Upper Midwest.

5. *Heart of Darkness* is:
   A self-help book about depression.
   b. A symbol-laden novella in which white men penetrate the darkest jungles of Africa and discover either the meaning of life or madness, depending on the man.
   c. A book about the making of Apocalypse Now.

6. *The Strange Case of Dr. Jekyll and Mr. Hyde* is:
   a. A Movie of the Week about a suicidal schizophrenic with an accompanying pattern of substance abuse.
   b. A novella that explores good and evil and their struggle for supremacy in the heart of every human being.
   c. A Movie of the Week about two hippies who took drugs and accidentally turned into businessmen and decided to make ice cream in Vermont.

7. *Nausea* is:
   a. A symbol of depression.
   b. A French existentialist novel whose main character experiences a lack of any real meaning in life.
   c. A symptom of pregnancy.

8. *Frankenstein* is:

a. What The Prince turns into if you let him move in.

b. A novel about the danger of humans playing God.

c. An upcoming Spielberg film about DNA research gone haywire.

9. *To Kill a Mockingbird* is:

a. A new self-help technique to overcome unwanted voices in one's head by throwing rocks at songbirds, which works by giving the user the experience of exercising control of his or her aural environment.

b. A novel about bigotry and justice.

c. A movie about a righteous southern lawyer with a daughter named Scout and really weird neighbors, the weirdest of whom turns out to be Robert Duvall in his first screen role.

10. *A Farewell to Arms* is:

a. A new self-help book that explains that women have a lot of problems in our male-dominated society because men have much more upper body strength than women. The solution is for women to forget about upper body strength (hence the title), and concentrate on toning their thighs. The blockbuster companion volume, for men who are willing to look at how they have used their upper body strength to oppress women, is called Arms and the Man.

b. A novel with the message that war is hell and so are relationships.

c. A radical eco-pacifist group in the Pacific Northwest.

Andra Douglas

Jennifer Camper

A HOUSE IS NOT A HOMO

by Jorjet Harper

The earliest word I ever heard used to refer to gays when I was a kid was "homo." I was about eight. My parents would say, in a disparaging way, how "the homos" did this, and "the homos" were like that.

We lived in a tiny, run-down, rented tenement apartment in New York. When my parents spoke derisively about the "the homos," I got the idea that they were talking about people who owned their own homes—that *homo* was short for *homeowner.*

I interpreted their negativity as jealousy. After all, who wouldn't want to be a homo? Homos had lots of room, sometimes little backyards and gardens. Lots of kids at school had parents who were homos. And there were quite a few homos living in row houses up the street.

My parents did own a television—and the TV shows were full of homos, too. *Father Knows Best, Leave it to Beaver*—even the *Beverly Hillbillies* were homos. The only people who weren't homos were Lucy & Desi (and what a spectacular apartment they had, by our standards), and the Kramdens on the *Jackie Gleason Show*, who lived in an apartment kind of like ours, only their kitchen was bigger.

Politicians, celebrities—it appeared that everybody who was anybody was a homo. Eventually my misunderstanding of the word became apparent. I called a few married people homos, to my parents' horror, and they questioned me till they figured out what I had meant to say.

"Well, what does homo mean, then?" I asked.

My parents looked at each other knowingly, as parents do.

"It's a boy who likes boys," mother said curtly, frowning.

Astute readers will note at once the lesbian invisibility implicit in this euphemistic, misleading reply. Unlike Queen Victoria, my mother was well aware of the existence of lesbians—but more about that another time.

"Lots of boys like boys," I observed.

"No, no, she means fairies," said my father, making a face. "Homos are fairies." He looked at me as if that ended the matter.

Fairies? But I *loved* fairies! My favorite childhood story was Peter Pan. And when Tinkerbell was dying, I clapped along with all the other kids, "I believe, I believe"—even though secretly I had a doubt or two.

"Men who act like fairies," my mother clarified. "Queens."

"Fairy Queens?!" I shouted with enthusiasm.

"No! No!" my mother shouted back. "Look, just stop calling Mr. and Mrs. Hamby up the street 'homos', alright? Don't use that word anymore."

"Alright then, but if you won't explain what it means, you can't say it either," I said sulking. "That's only fair."

Since they really didn't want to delve any deeper into the subject, they agreed. There was no more talk about "the homos"—at least not in front of me. They took the home out of homophobia, but not the homophobia out of the home.

We can be pretty complicated, perplexing creatures we Homo sapiens.

HEROINES WE CAN LIVE WITH

by Ellen Orleans

Lesbian Adventure Novels? Well, with summer just around the corner, it's time to break out that bottle of sparkling soda, climb into a hammock or spread a blanket in the park, and settle into a solid stack of lesbian fiction. So, with the the wealth of genius out there, what's on the best seller list? Detective novels. And murder mysteries. And crime thrillers.

Now look, I enjoy escapism and adventure as much as the next gal, but I'd like to see a little realism now and then. Not all of us are travel agents turned crime solvers, or out-of-work English majors who just sort of fell into the private-eye business. I believe that some realistic, true-to-life adventure is in order. Therefore, I present the first in a collection of *Ellen's Get Real, Real Life Challenges*, adventure series.

Margie Biblin: Vet Tech! Follow the harrowing and heartwarming tales of veterinarian technician Margie Biblin as she narrowly escapes the jaws of injured canines atop examining room tables, expertly dodges vicious claws while administering feline-leukemia shots, or makes the soul-searching, life-changing decision to adopt an abandoned three-legged rabbit into her life. Whether it's soothing frantic pet owners, or selflessly giving up that one quiet evening at home to dole out free medical advice to friends too broke to make a real appointment, *Margie Biblin: Vet Tech!* is sure to inspire animal lovers and adventure seekers everywhere.

Psychologist's Girlfriend: The True Story of Sylvia Sanchez. Being the girlfriend of a clinical psychologist is an even greater challenge than passing the bar exam, Sylvia Sanchez discovers in this gripping, first-person narrative. You too will writhe in frustration as you watch Sylvia and girlfriend Tanya give up social event after social event just to avoid seeing Tanya's clients. When Tanya calls ahead to compare guest list to client list before attending the hottest housewarming in all of Seattle, will Sylvia strike out on her own and go alone? Or will she stay home and rationalize that she needed to review those briefs anyway? What fine line separates professional protocol and a meaningful social life? And just how far will they go to stay together?

Terry Yakamoto: Adventures of a Reluctant Suburban Dyke. After the untimely death of her parents, Terry unexpectedly finds herself responsible for, and living in, her New Jersey split-level childhood home. While waiting for the lawyers, relatives and debtors to settle their differences, Terry attempts to keep alive a new, long-distance relationship, modem rewrites to her office and illegally sublet her rent-controlled apartment in the city. And when it all takes a metaphysical turn as Terry experiences the ghosts of her parents, while driving in their late-model minivan in search of a six-pack of decent beer, we see that the suburban search for meaning is just beginning.

Jolyne MacCray Takes on the Collective. It's a rough ride for European-American sociology professor and disabilities rights activist Jolyne MacCray. With her lover Elena off to Liberia on a Rhodes Scholarship and best friend Rosa on a whirlwind book tour, Jolyne learns she has been denied tenure by a stodgy group of male professors. Retreating to a small women's college for the summer, Jolyne thinks immersing herself in the lesbian community will ease her pain. But watch out...these microbiotic, newspaper-recycling lesbians prove that white privilege and ableism is alive and well and raging at the Collective. Can Jolyne get through to the seemingly oblivious feminists without the help of Rosa and Elena? Will Elena's latest book, delayed at the printer's, arrive in time to educate, enlighten and prevent a murder? Or will Jolyne finally take an ax to the collective's bathroom, making it truly accessible once and for all?

Vengeful Spirit. When eternal graduate student and visiting house guest LouAnne takes it upon herself to point out all the differences between lesbian (over)activist Lucy and her cable-T.V.-addicted girlfriend Lonnie, all hell breaks loose...until the three of them discover there's a ghost in the house. Or is the "ghost" a prank of the local religious right group who hope to derail Lucy's latest plans for a local lesbian cable network? Can everyone work together, or is one of the three not who she appears to be?

Yup, looks like we have a fine summer of reading lined up here. So pass the mineral water and sink into—well, if it's not exactly reality—maybe a little escapism isn't so bad after all.

Kate Debold

"Her books might be trash, but she sure knows how to promote them!"

LYDIA'S ISLE

by Carolyn Parkhurst

Theme Song:
Just sit right back, and you'll hear a tale,
The tale of a sapphic trip—
It started from the 70s
Bound for Lesbos on this ship.
The separatists said "Break away
From patriarchal lore!"
Six lesbians set sail that day
To find something more
To find something more.
The ship set ground on the shore of this
Uncharted desert isle
With Lydia,
Her lover Lu,
The 50s butch and her femme,
The baby dyke,
The professor and not one man,
Here on Lydia's Isle!

Closing Theme:
No whips, no chains, no motorbikes,
Our gynecocracy,
Fighting for a different world,
Utopian as can be.
So join us here each week, my friends,
You're sure to get a smile
From six wacky separatists
Here on Lydia's Isle!

Viv Quillin

Rina Piccolo

Karen Brown

CITY of CONNUBIAL MISS LOVE™

EVERYBODY SAYS THE *FIRST YEAR* OF MARRIAGE IS THE *HARDEST*...

MUST BE *RIGHT UP THERE*.

BUT I KINDA THINK THE *LAST YEAR*...

©1993 K. BROWN

YOU'RE BOYCOTTING GRANDMA'S WEDDING BECAUSE LESBIANS CAN'T MARRY? WHY WOULD YOU EVEN WANT TO MARRY? LESBIANS CAN'T PROCREATE.

EVER AFTER

by May Richstone

She felt lovely, O so cherished!
He felt lucky, ten feet tall!
Togetherness was very heaven —
Then they got married and spoiled it all.

Signe Wilkinson

In Our Opinion

Shary Flenniken

Viv Quillin

"I now pronounce you, HOUSE and WIFE."

FLASHPOINT *by Flash Rosenberg*

• We don't celebrate our birthday before we're born.

• We don't graduate on the first day of school.

• We don't win gold medals before the race.

1st

SO WHY ON EARTH DO WE HAVE WEDDINGS?

"I DO"...(NOT UNDERSTAND).....

Weddings are the **ONLY** *occasion celebrated* **BEFORE THE FACT.**

©1990

Flash Rosenberg

Marian Henley

Jennifer Berman

WHEN DAD DATES: THE POTENTIAL STEPMOTHER
TRUE STORIES BY JUDY BECKER
c.1992
#1: POST-TRAUMA BOMBSHELL:
MEAT?
DO WE HAVE TO EAT IT?
LOOKS GREAT, HONEYBUNS
CLOTHES SHE PICKED OUT
EAT UP, KIDS, HOPE YA LIKE PORK!
TOTALLY UNHIP CLOTHES IN 1971
WE HAVE A PORTO RICAN MAID!
YEAH. THEY CALL THEM SPICS CAUSE THEY NO SPIC ENGLISH!
HA HA HA
(OUR FUTURE STEP-BROTHER + SISTER)
I CAN'T BELIEVE SHE SERVED FROZEN PEAS! THAT'S SO UNNATURAL!
YEAH, AND DAD SAID SHE WAS THE JEANS AND T-SHIRT TYPE. HE DIDN'T MENTION THE JEANS WERE PINK WITH RHINESTONES
THEY BROKE UP WHEN SHE INSISTED ON MARRIAGE

continued...

THE POTENTIAL STEPMOTHER #2: BRAINY PRUDE
JUDY (YES, MY NAMESAKE!) WAS A PSYCHIATRIC SOCIAL WORKER SPECIALIZING IN CHILDREN. SHE HAD NO IDEA HER SON WAS THE BIGGEST DOPE DEALER IN SCHOOL.
AND MY SON JOHNATHAN IS SUCH A GENTLEMAN- AND A WONDERFUL VIOLINIST
THATS NICE
YEAH YEAH- LETS SEE THE BREAD
ARE YOU SURE ITS REAL HASH?
* JOHNNY ENDED UP IN JAIL AND HAS RECENTLY BEEN MARKETING HIMSELF AS A REHABILITATED EX-CON VIOLINIST.
MY MOST MEMORABLE ENCOUNTER WITH HER:
(STUPIDLY CONFIDING IN HER)
YOU KNOW, I CAN'T WAIT TILL I FALL IN LOVE. I'M REALLY CURIOUS ABOUT SEX, BUT I WANT IT TO BE SPECIAL THE FIRST TIME
WELL, HAVING LOST YOUR MOTHER, ITS OBVIOUS YOU JUST WANT SEX AS A SUBSTITUTE FOR MATERNAL AFFECTION. I UNDERSTAND ALL THIS - I'VE BEEN ANALYZED MYSELF. NOT THAT THE ANALYST TOLD ME ANYTHING I DIDN'T ALREADY KNOW.
TAB WITH LEMON
THEY BROKE UP WHEN SHE INSISTED ON MARRIAGE- SHE WROTE HIM RANTING LETTERS FOR YEARS AFTER.

continued...

POTENTIAL STEPMOTHER #3: THE ONE THAT GOT HIM
YEAH RIGHT
I'VE ALWAYS BEEN INDEPENDENT. I FIND IT PATHETIC WHEN WOMEN RELY ON MEN FOR THEIR HAPPINESS BLAH BLAH BLAH*
LILI'S REALLY SOMETHING, ISN'T SHE!
UH HUH
WILL YOU MARRY ME?
NO, I'M NOT READY FOR THAT KIND OF COMMITMENT
*HAS NEVER BEEN WITHOUT A MAN IN HER LIFE!
SIX MONTHS LATER:
LOOK WHO FINALLY SAID YES!
JUST THINK OF ME AS A FRIEND, NOT A STEPMOTHER
OH NO
AFTER THE WEDDING:
ALRIGHT KIDS-THERE'S GONNA BE SOME CHANGES AROUND HERE!
SEE ANY TRADITIONAL FAIRYTALE FOR REST OF THE STORY

JACKET PRAISES

by Flash Rosenberg

I just finished reading a book I liked so much
that I read all the jacket praises
when I ran out of book
just to make it last a little longer.
Oh, if only men had praises on their jackets, just like books.
"A witty romp." "Impossible to put down." "A real tear-jerker."
Then there'd still be something to read
when he no longer lets you read him.
Something to scan during dinner, say,
when you're just trying to hold your place.
And make it last a little longer.

Stephanie Piro

"We were out testing his tosterone... he passed!"

I KNOW HOW TO FIX THE WORLD!

by Dianne Reum

With the exception of Addy (my two-year-old buddy who thinks I am Super Woman) (probably because of the tights and cape), I'm sure no one ever dreamed it would be me, Dianne Reum, who would discover the solution to rape, the abortion issue, violent crimes, *and* war.

But I have.

The answer came to me while I was staying at a friend's house. Princess Bob helped me to find it.

Princess Bob is brimming with love—he adores all the members of his household, all strangers who enter his home (even Bush-voting Republicans), and a possum who lumbers into his backyard from time to time.

Princess Bob is a snow-white neutered cat, one of the six animals (four cats and two large dogs) my friend has.

It was while Princess Bob, one of the dogs and I were sitting on the back porch, sponging in sunshine, that Princess Bob helped me see the solution. As I sat watching Princess Bob lazily lick the dog, I thought two things: 1) I wish someone were licking me, and 2) castration does wonders for a male's attitude.

At that moment I realized it would be a truly groovy world (and I mean "groovy" in the most spiritual sense) if all belligerent, narrow-minded and combative men were castrated, like Princess Bob. Only men, who women allowed steering wheels, would have sex drives. These select men would be compassionate, intelligent and gentle. (And would know how to dress.) (There must be a couple hundred who aren't gay.)

Many men obviously fancy themselves not far removed from tomcats, with their expressions "on the prowl," "piece of tail," "fur-burger" and "pussy." Even those good Christian men (self-proclaimed) who say "wooing," "intercourse," "private parts," and "down *there,*" with their crusades against abortion, think they have some animalistic right to sink their claws into our uteri.

Too often men have been looking for ways to control women, when men have been peeing on the carpet of life and sharpening their claws on the sofas of our hearts.

I say let's get the ball rolling and get their balls rolling. (Men will only fight us on this until they've had the operations.)

There must be a reason that, for as long as I can remember, people have been referring to castrating animals as "having them fixed".

Pat Horner

He <u>SAYS</u> no, but does he really <u>MEAN</u> no?

Cath Jackson

Gail Machlis

MINS MOVEMENT?

by Hattie Gossett

what? a mins movement? what you mean a mins movement? ain't they still runnin the world? what they need a movement for? what? is this some kind of a joke about laxatives or something? bashing? oh—bashing? theyre trying to heal the cruel wounds of mins bashing? wait a minute—did i miss something? do they have to wear breast implants false fingernails get paid less money have no power & get whistled at? do they? huh? huh?

well what do they mean? whatre they going to the woods for then? oh? really? sensitive? does that mean theyre against rape now? when they come back from the woods do they issue statements against child abuse wife battering incest lesbian battering? do they pledge that the next time one of their streetcorner or healthclub buddies is running off at the mouth about how he snatched him some pussy then kicked that bitch in her ass these guys who paid all this money to go to the woods with whats his name will they silently organize a small group to take their brother for a little walk & show him some tongue and penis restraint exercises guaranteed to permanently clear his mind of all thoughts of ripping off pussy or bitches or kicking ass?

no? what you mean not exactly? well whatre they going to the woods for then? is it to get in touch with their homoerotic selves? to discover the queens within? to stop worrying about the size of their dicks? not exactly? what? playing drums? dancing around the fire? camping out? is this some more pseudo tribal stuff? a revised ersatz "heart of darkness" number? a bunch of boys playing games with the cultures of people they don't know how to live next door to?

Gail Machlis

HOW CAN I GET MORNING SICKNESS WHEN I DON'T GET UP TILL NOON?

by Rita Rudner

I know lots of women have had children. I've seen them—both the women who have had them and the children they have had. But I'm not sure it's for me. Some women glow, they radiate, they incandesce (and that isn't even a word) when they are pregnant.

"Feel the baby kicking, feel the baby kicking," says my friend who is six minutes pregnant and deliriously happy about it. To me, life is tough enough without having someone kick you from the inside.

Upon finding out the test strip turned bluish, yellowish green, my friend (let's call her "Jeremiah," because I don't know anyone called that and I don't want any of my friends to be mad at me) immediately bought one of those books that have pictures of what the baby is doing every day. (I'm not sure it's entirely accurate—in one photo the baby is playing cards.)

"Look at its little veins and fingers and feet," she says.

continued...

I feign interest while feeling sick and say, "And I think it has gin."

She looks at me strangely, because I have imagined the photo of the baby playing cards, because I was so bored. Jeremiah kicks me out of her house for not taking the development of her child seriously enough. Jeremiah never could take a joke.

Another friend (for variety's sake I'll call this friend "Phleghh") is a frontier woman. I'm not Danielle Boone. I've never done drugs in my life, but if I ever did have a baby, at that point I would say, "Shoot me up." To me natural childbirth is backward; nowadays everyone takes drugs except when they need them. Phleghh didn't even want to have her baby in a hospital. She preferred a hut. The more mud the better. She didn't want a doctor, either. She wanted a squaw. Phleghh settled on a hospital that was painted taupe and a doctor who liked Dances With Wolves. Phleghh was in labor for thirty-six hours. (I don't even want to do anything that feels good for thirty-six hours.) The baby was turned the wrong way. Phleghh had the choice of a cesarean with drugs or writhing in pain in the hope that her unborn child would obtain a sense of direction. Phleghh wanted a cesarean without drugs. I think at this point the unborn child had pity and did an Olga Korbut-like flip. Phleghh is happy and proud that she didn't resort to drugs, but she never did have another baby. Phleghh's baby is now sixteen and does drugs.

It's clear that nature was not altogether fair to women regarding the childbearing process. Other species seem luckier. There's a bird right outside my window that I've been watching as I've been working on this book. She laid some eggs that were an entirely reasonable size, and in a few days they hatched. The results are cute, and now she brings them food. I could deal with that.

Envy the kangaroo. That pouch setup is extraordinary; the baby crawls out of the womb when it is about two inches long, gets into the pouch, and proceeds to mature. I'd have a baby if it would develop in my handbag. The dolphin just mocks us. I saw a dolphin give birth, and it didn't even stop swimming. It had a baby while working out! Talk about an overachiever.

I know there are all these new and wonderful birthing methods where you put the baby in water or lay it on your stomach and pour warm mushroom-barley soup over it to ease the poor unsuspecting thing into the real world. I'm in favor of a more straightforward approach to life; I think the delivery room should have traffic noise and pollution, and you should immediately put the baby on the phone and have someone be rude to it. The baby should then have the option to go back in.

I guess what I'm trying to say is that some women are cut out for motherhood and some aren't, and I don't know which type I am, but I just reread this chapter and I have a suspicion.

SOME TIPS FOR PREPARED CHILDREARING

by Cathy Crimmins

Everyone talks about prepared childbirth, but what about the next phase? Here are some steps you can take to get yourself ready for the days ahead.

Buy a box of Adult Size diapers and practice putting them on your husband.

Go through your closet and smear cream cheese on all your favorite blouses.

During the day: Put a timer on for 4 minutes; when it goes off, cease whatever you are doing—reading, cooking, making love, watching television, doing laundry—and run frantically to another room

At night: Set your alarm clock for every two hours. When it rings, make your husband get up to feed and burp the cat.

Jan Eliot

Chris Suddick

Gail Machlis

Margie Cherry

Karen Brown

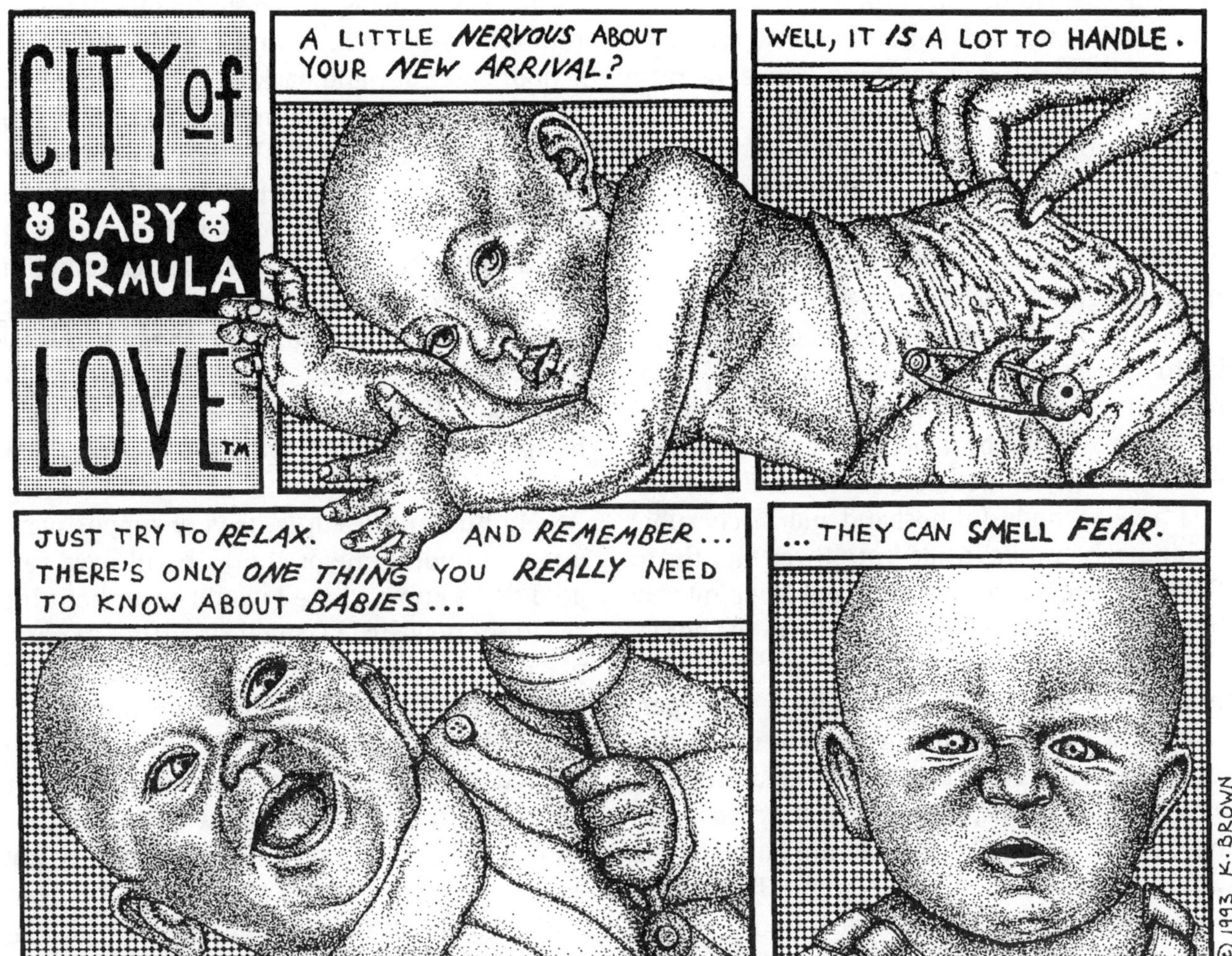
CITY of BABY FORMULA LOVE™
A LITTLE NERVOUS ABOUT YOUR NEW ARRIVAL?
WELL, IT IS A LOT TO HANDLE.
JUST TRY TO RELAX. AND REMEMBER... THERE'S ONLY ONE THING YOU REALLY NEED TO KNOW ABOUT BABIES...
... THEY CAN SMELL FEAR.
© 1993 K. BROWN

WHY I WOULD LIKE TO BE READER OF THE YEAR

by Melinda Brindley

I am a Better Homes and Women reader. I bake quite a lot—at least 10 different new recipes a day. But I never touch anything I bake, being a slim Better Woman. I send everything I bake to underdeveloped countries. Then I snack on my allotted broiled shark fins with a squeeze of lemon, sticking loyally to my weight loss regime. I've already lost 50 pounds in two weeks and feel so much lighter, especially in the head.

I make all my own clothes, and hope someday to own a sewing machine. Most people comment on my clothes with such envious remarks as, "You made that by hand, didn't you." I always blush modestly and confess that, yes, I did.

I have a wonderful husband and 17 cherubic children who range in age from three months to 17 years. They certainly keep me hopping. My husband believes a woman's place is in the home, a philosophy which I certainly share. Someday, though, I'd like to step outside for a walk, perhaps to the park or the liquor store, as my friends sometimes say I look pasty. My husband does help with the housework, though. By downright laying down the law, I've gotten him to place the dinner dishes in the sink every night. This makes it so much easier for me to wash them, as I no longer trip on my seven toddlers while bringing dishes from table to sink. I'm so glad, because two of the toddlers were taking it personally and are now seeing therapists.

Between caring for three infants and seven rambunctious tots, taking four of my kids to school every day and packing their lunches, and listening to the woes of my 14- and 15-year-old girls, as well as visiting the 17-year-old at High House, I'm one busy lady. (We discovered last year that my 17-year-old is a pothead and, darn it, I'm not ashamed to admit it. We suspected something when he stopped speaking except for an occasional obscenity, but the turning point in our lives was when he made us all some brownies and we were soon stoned out of our minds. Then we knew he had a problem and we did something about it.)

My husband, George, is very supportive, always reminding me of chores I still have yet to do. I don't know where I would be without him.

Right now, little Danielle is sitting in my lap, playing with the typewriter *()!Z#@ what a little handful she is. Uh-oh—trouble upstairs.

I'm back. Timmy was letting the dog walk on his bed, which he had covered with peanut butter and jelly. He loves peanut butter and jelly. Well, I put the dog outside, but now I've got a wall to wash because Timmy stuck the peanut butter-smeared sheet to it. At least he's healthy. I keep reminding myself of that.

Got to go—Bobby is beating his sister senseless with a nerf bat. And Joey is trying to unplug this typew

Lynn Johnson

Jan Eliot

the art of motherhood

MOM'S MAIL-ORDER MIRACLES

HOLIDAY GIFTS WE'D REALLY LIKE !!!

ITEM 1A

NOW YOU CAN HOLD 2 KIDS, THE GROCERIES, AND PUSH A STROLLER! THE POSSIBILITIES ARE ENDLESS! $40.

1B

THEY HOLD THE PHONE WHILE YOU CHANGE THE BABY, DO THE DISHES, OR TIE SHOELACES. A MUST FOR BUSY MOMS! $20.

BUY BOTH... SAVE $5.!

ITEM 2A

SHE'S EFFICIENT, RELIABLE, PATIENT, & PLAYFUL... EVERYTHING YOU'RE NOT! ONLY $75.

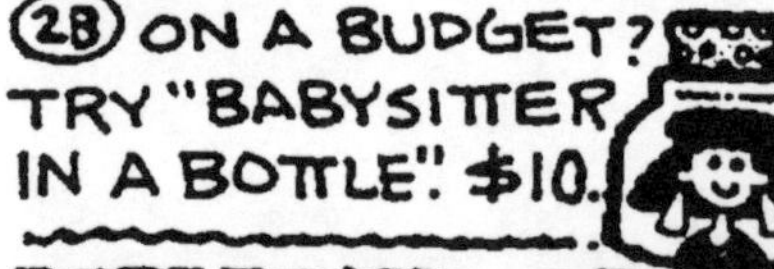

ITEM 3

JUST WHAT YOU'VE BEEN ASKING FOR! 12 EXTRA HOURS FOR YOUR BUSY DAY $36.

THE BIG BOOK OF WHY ?

4

3,000 PAGES OF ANSWERS FOR EVERY "WHY?" A TODDLER CAN ASK!! ONLY $20.

HOLIDAY SPECIAL!

HAS HOLIDAY SHOPPING WITH THE KIDS SHORTENED YOUR TEMPER? TRY OUR NEW "TEMPER EXTENSION CORD" 99¢

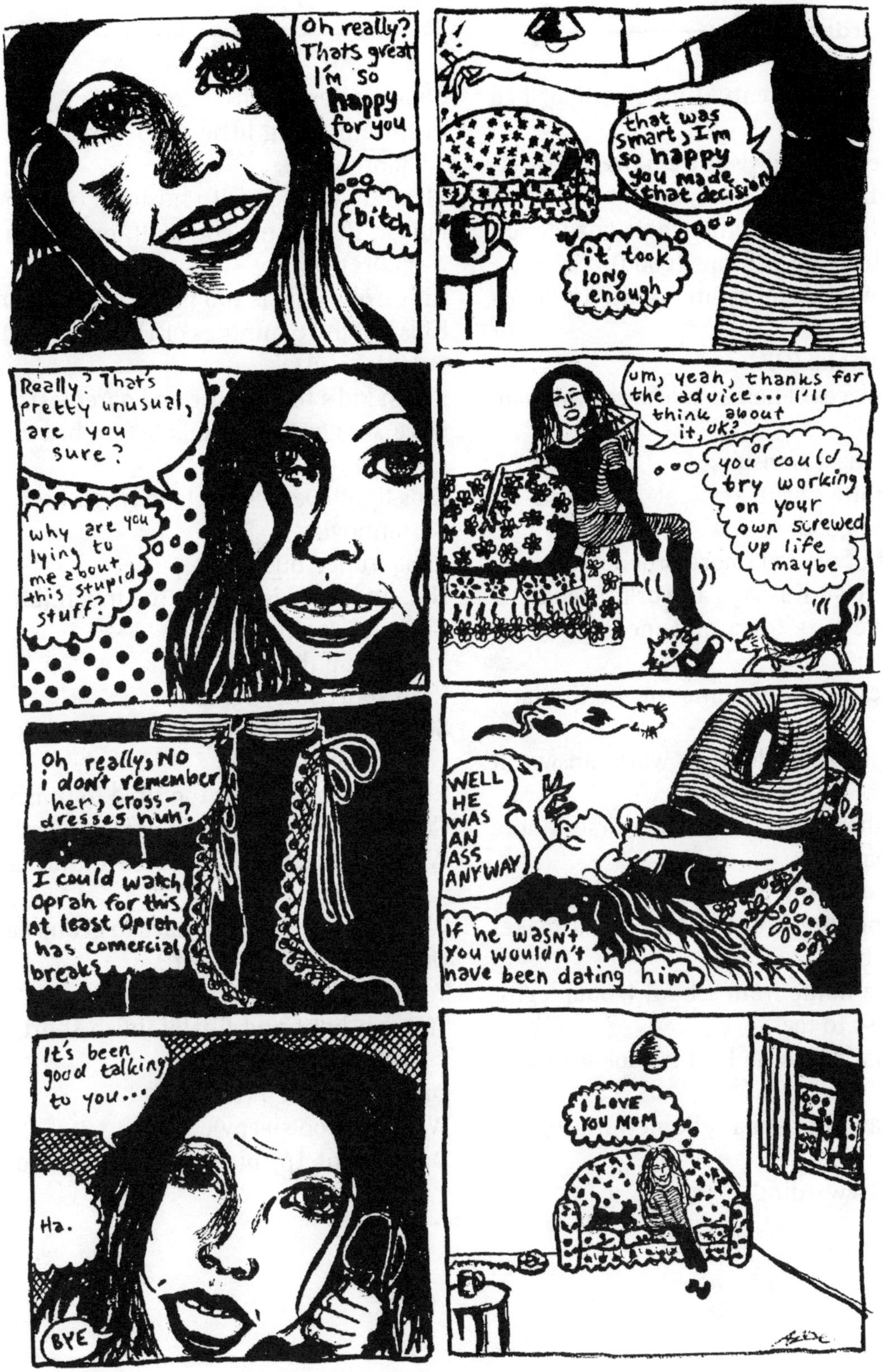

Oh really? Thats great I'm so **happy** for you

bitch

that was smart, I'm so **happy** you made that decision

it took long enough

Really? That's pretty unusual, are you sure?

why are you lying to me about this stupid stuff?

um, yeah, thanks for the advice... I'll think about it, OK?

or you could try working on your own screwed up life maybe

oh really, NO i don't remember her, cross-dresses huh?

I could watch oprah for this at least Oprah has comercial breaks

WELL HE WAS AN ASS ANYWAY

If he wasn't you wouldn't have been dating him

It's been good talking to you...

Ha.

BYE

CHOICES

by Nicole S. Urdang

Don't want to, but eventually get out of bed (good).
Pour Rice Chex into bowls for children's breakfasts (good).
Resist temptation to scarf the whole box (good).
Force myself to swim 108 laps (good).
Chew the fat with locker room cronies (procrastinating).
Breakfast: ravenous (OK).
Eat two huge pieces of homemade bread with jam (healthy).
But while the toast's crisping
Nuke some coffee cake and eat that (bad—it wasn't even good).
Read 50 pages of a novel (more procrastination).
Go upstairs to visit husband at work (friendly).
Turn down overture for a mid-morning romp (stupid).
Read a fan letter from someone in England (great).
Rather than get right down to work, answer it (bad).
Take care of other correspondence (worse—more procrastination).
Eat a clementine from Morocco (healthy).
Put some lemon/fig bread in the bread maker (good and bad).
Children come home from school (good, legitimate excuse to loaf).
Give children a snack and eat a cookie (not so good).
Check over daughter's math homework (parental).
See a patient (rewarding).
Cook dinner (good).
Keep reminding little son to lean over his plate (annoying).
Clean up kitchen with husband (routine).
Put on Peter And The Wolf for kids to frolic to (cute).
Kids frolic a little too much (annoying).
Kids watch 15 minutes of TV and I read the paper (peaceful).
Brush kid's teeth (cute and parental).
Have songfest with kids before bed (sweet, until...)
Kids fight over who gets to sing which song first (annoying).
All is ironed out (OK).
Hug and kiss kids much too much (blissful).
Go to bedroom (good).
Put feet up (better).
Read short story (great).
Son interrupts with request for extra kisses (manipulated).
Read story again but too tired to finish it (bad).
Go downstairs for frozen yogurt (good).
Watch Masterpiece Theatre with husband in bed (great).
Want to make love but have to get up early (bad).
Do it anyway (energized).
Too keyed up to sleep (annoyed).
Turn on light and finally finish short story (accomplished).
Drop off to sleep (too late).
Wake up (too sleepy).
Don't want to, but eventually get out of bed (good).

CONGRATULATIONS ON YOUR PROMOTION, MS. KIRKPATRICK!
$15,000 RAISE AND A KEY TO THE EXECUTIVE GYM~
WHO SAYS A WOMAN CAN'T HAVE IT ALL?
I PHONED THE BABYSITTER AND MADE RESERVATIONS AT LA TROMPERIE~LET'S CELEBRATE MY PROMOTION IN STYLE!!
I'M JUST TOO BUSHED TO GO OUT TONIGHT, DOLL. GET ROSA TO HELP YOU FIX SOMETHING NICE HERE...
GRIM REPORTS FROM EL SALVADOR.. REFUGEES FLEE... REAGANS ORDER NEW THRONES...
SHARON RUDAHL©1984
I'M RAISING YOUR PAY TO $100 A WEEK, ROSA~ AND HERE ARE SOME OLD TOYS OF DANI'S FOR YOUR GIRLS!
MUCHAS GRACIAS, MADAM...
SUNNY DAY, CHASING YOUR CARES AWAY...
CAREER WOMAN ROSA, WHOSE HUSBAND DIDN'T MAKE IT ACROSS THE BORDER, PAYS OUT HALF HER SALARY TO THE WEE WINKIE DAY CARE CENTER.
COUGH! COUGH!
NO, NO!! NOT WHILE HE'S IN A COMA!
BUS
IF YOU'RE LATE AGAIN, MRS., I GOT TO CHARGE EXTRA.
MAMA!!
MAMA!
...P, FOR PEOPLE IN OUR NEIGHBORHOOD!
LMNOP
WHAT DID YOU LEARN TODAY?

WHEN YOUR TEENAGER LACKS AMBITION

by May Richstone

Don't fret, instead
Just look ahead—
He'll do you proud
After you're dead.

Jane Caminos

Rina Piccolo

CONUNDRUM

by Lois Green Stone

Run the circular track in a schoolyard,
Or in park on a trail that's all dirt.
I've a choice: to be bored in a circle
Or be free for the muggers to hurt.

Dianne Reum

Nina's Adventures
©Nina Paley '91
GASP! CHOKE!
EXCUSE ME, COULD YOU PLEASE PUT OUT YOUR CIGARETTE?
HEY BUDDY, THIS IS AMERICA AND IT'S MY RIGHT-NAY, MY DUTY-TO EXHALE SMOKE ALL OVER YOUR MEAL!
UH-OH!
THIS LOOKS LIKE A JOB FOR...
LADIES
MILITANT ANTISMOKING WOMAN!!
OH NO! IT'S MILITANT ANTISMOKING WOMAN!!
BOOT!
CHOP!
STOMP STOMP STOMP
KILL KILL KILL
SWOON! MY HEROINE!
JUST PART OF A DAY'S WORK FOR MILITANT ANTISMOKING WOMAN!!
The End (DON'T I WISH!)
Nina's Adventures
©Nina Paley 2-22-92
I FEEL ANGRY.
WHAT?! I DIDN'T DO ANYTHING WRONG!
I DIDN'T SAY YOU DID.
DID SO! YOU JUST ACCUSED ME OF DOING SOMETHING WRONG!
NO, I SAID I FELT ANGRY.
WELL STOP TRYING TO CHANGE MY BEHAVIOR! I DON'T CARE IF I DID DO SOMETHING WRONG!
THE BUDDHA WOULDN'T LET HIMSELF GET ANGRY!
TAKE RESPONSIBILITY FOR YOUR OWN FEELINGS AND STOP TRYING TO CONTROL ME!
YOU MUST BE INSECURE!
ARE YOU SAYING YOU DON'T WANT TO BE FRIENDS ANY MORE? WELL FINE!
BOY DO YOU HAVE A PROBLEM WITH ANGER!

ANGER

by Sara Cytron and Harriet Malinowitz

One thing we've learned from feminist therapists is that a lot of women have trouble getting in touch with their anger. But one thing these therapists don't realize is that none of these women live in New York. In New York, we're all in touch with our anger.

Like let's say it's a rainy day, and you're coming out of the subway, and somebody opens up their umbrella, and it hits you in the side of the head. Now I don't know about the rest of the country, but any self-respecting New York woman is going to say: "Will you fucking watch what you're doing?"

But let's say it's another rainy day, and you're coming out of the subway, and this time it's you opening up the umbrella, and you hit somebody else in the head, and they say "Will you fucking watch what you're doing?" Of course, you're going to say: "For Christ's sake, can't you tell it was a fucking accident?"

I spent a lot of last summer in Provincetown, Massachusetts and it was very easy to tell the New York dykes on vacation in Provincetown. They're the ones that if you accidentally brush against them in the water, they say: "What's a matter? Ocean's not big enough for you?!"

New Yorkers, relaxing, on vacation.

Jackie Urbanovic

Mary Lawton

Jennifer Berman

Jan Eliot

THE NEXT TIME SOMEONE CALLS ME 'SWEETHEART' I'M GOING TO SCREAM !!
CRASH!

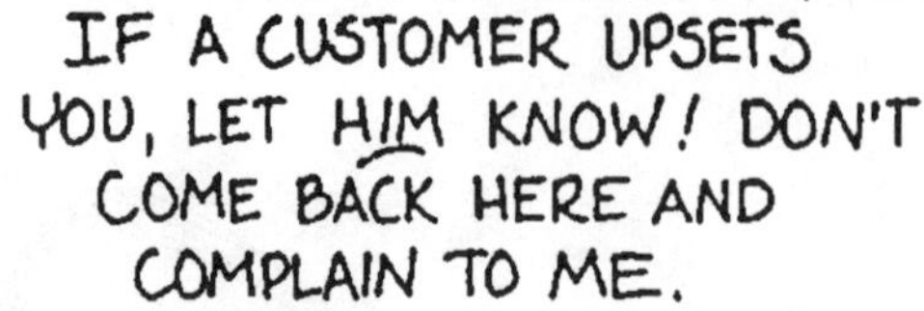
IF A CUSTOMER UPSETS YOU, LET HIM KNOW! DON'T COME BACK HERE AND COMPLAIN TO ME.

GRRR

YOU'VE GOT TO LEARN TO DEAL WITH YOUR ANGER MORE DIRECTLY !!

BETTER, BUT A LITTLE TOO IMPULSIVE.
©Jan Eliot

TURTLES, BEARS & YAKS

Rina Piccolo

TURTLE ON THE LAM

by Adair Lara

I didn't mean to lose the turtle. It's just that since Neil and I had this fight, I've had to work brooding into an already crowded schedule, and I completely forgot that I put the turtle in the yard.

We just got him last weekend. Seventy bucks for one five-inch turtle with accessories, including a glass aquarium and a dozen feeder goldfish. Despite this largess, the turtle seemed depressed and was spending all day staring moodily through the glass.

Thinking a little constitutional would cheer him up, I plopped him down by the rosebush and went in the house to vacuum the ants out of the freezer and run a speculative finger across the topsoil on the venetian blinds. Then it was time to brood about Neil for a while. By the time I remembered Todd—short for Todd Turtle—and raced outside, he was gone—a lean green escaping machine.

I don't think he was justified in taking off. There should be such a thing as commitment, even for turtles. Besides, I liked the little guy. The kids had fallen in love with his fish dinners, giving them names like Spud and Tiny and putting them in cereal bowls, but I had bonded with Todd. He was slow in more ways than one — in a classroom where the seating is by IQ, turtles would sit right in front of salamanders — but he reminded me of Neil. Maybe it was the way he would go into his shell sometimes. At least in Todd's case you could see him doing it — you just glanced over to see if his head was there or not.

Besides, I have money invested here. Todd is worth $15 on the — what? Not hoof. What are turtle feet called? Hold on, I'll look it up. A little turtle research might take my mind off Neil. Patrick asked whether the turtle came with instructions (city kid), so I got this book called *Turtles*.

Here it is. How to operate your turtle. But there's nothing on what turtle feet are called.

Wait, here's something else. "Turtles do not pair for life or even for a season. A male finds a female who acts or looks or smells right and he rubs her face with his long claws or bites her legs, and eventually she may become receptive."

"Acts or looks or smells right"? He just nibbles her feet, whatever the hell they're called, and she melts? I had no idea girl turtles were this shallow.

This is working. I have pretty much forgotten about what's his name. Still perplexed about Todd, though. Might have to get a plaque out there, dedicated to the Old Turtle, whose fate we shall never know. "He just marched off one morning, without a word to anyone, and the waters of history closed over his little green head." Either that or he's hiding in the ivy by the brick wall, congratulating himself on his cleverness and planning the next stage, a sprint into the Nakamuras' yard.

He would do better to just come on back. I can't offer him a goldfish—they are all swimming around in my dinnerware—but we do have that great staple of turtle cuisine, Tetra Repto Min Floating Food Sticks. Todd is the same bilious green as every plant in my garden, and so stands a good chance of being discarded by the teenager who's coming over in a little while to pull weeds. Even the Old Gringo didn't have to go out to face his maker in a brown plastic bag with bits of hedge and rosemary.

Could be worse, though. Listen to this: "If your turtle is sick and past saving, the humane way to kill it is to seal it in a plastic bag and put it in the freezer."

I can just see this. Neil comes over, begging forgiveness for momentarily forgetting how wonderful I am. I manage to pluck his name out of the air and offer to make him dinner. "Honey, what do you feel like eating?" I'll ask.

"Oh, I don't know," he'll say. "Why don't you defrost something?"

Rina Piccolo

Paula Peters

PP

THERE'S ONLY ONE DIFFERENCE BETWEEN AN ELEPHANT AND AN OLDER MAN. ONE IS A DIMWITTED OVERWEIGHT BEAST WHO SHOWS OFF WITH HIS TRUNK. THE OTHER IS A CIRCUS ANIMAL.

YOSEMITE BEARS

by Judy MacLean

The Yosemite ranger wore the cheery expression common to those who commune with the wilderness by dispensing triplicate forms eight hours a day. He was exhorting me and my backpacking partner, Leanne, to cooperate with the new bear policy.

The old policy was roughly this: as thousands of humans streamed into the Yosemite back country, bent under the weight of a smorgasbord of treats especially tempting to the ursine palate, we were supposed to deceive the bears into believing we weren't there. We sneakily hid our food in trees at night. We never took so much as an M&M into our tents, so as not to attract a shaggy nocturnal nosher. We left no crumbs around the campfire. In fact, we built no campfire. Instead, we packed in a tiny gas stove. This allowed what little deadwood is left in Yosemite to rot on the ground, to convince both ourselves and the bears that a lake the size of a basketball court surrounded by forty tents constitutes a pristine wilderness. We left only footsteps and took only photos.

All this was supposed to teach the bears to resist the temptation to ruin their health with the Hershey bars, parmesan and smoked salmon dangling from the trees, gift-wrapped in ripstop nylon. The bears were supposed to stay in the bushes, rustling up appropriate fare like ants, thimbleberries and mice.

I can't imagine why the rangers decided to change the old policy. It worked perfectly. It gave everyone who packed into Yosemite a tale to tell back in the city: the bear who lolled at the edge of the Tuolumne River, sensuously licking powdered milk from its paws; the bear who strolled into camp every night around dinnertime, forcing the trailblazers to race away balancing a bubbling pot of reconstituted freeze-dried Turkey Tetrazzini; the bear who didn't get the food, but shredded a $200 backpack in pursuing a tube of toothpaste. Under the old policy, bears cut short thousands of expeditions, reducing the human impact on Yosemite's wilderness by tens of thousands of person-days. Plus, replacing bear-gnawed gear provided regular stimulation to the American economy. If that's not a successful policy, what is?

But bureaucrats will be bureaucrats, even if they are rangers, too. They can't leave well enough alone.

Luckily, the most fun part of the old policy had been carried over: counterbalancing our food for the night. This simple task involves finding a tree with a branch no shorter than a Cadillac, no thicker than a thumb, with no other branches close by, about 25 feet up. After you find it, throwing the required rope over it and rigging the food is no problem, as long as you have Dave Stewart's arm and Wilt Chamberlain's stature. Leanne and I can usually accomplish it in less than three hours, with fewer than four arguments about who broke the branch or got the rope terminally snarled.

Under the old policy, we were supposed to locate this branch at least a football field away from our campsite. This was to fool the four-footed gourmets into thinking food sacks and humans don't really travel together.

The new policy said to tie the food up in a tree close to the tent. As the optimistic ranger explained it, "Yosemite has only black bears, and they are basically timid. We need to teach them that we're the dominant species here."

And when the basically timid creatures wandered over to our food, the ranger instructed us to be ready to fight for it.

And so, as the sun set over Young Lake, and the golden moon peeked over the granite rampart on the far shore, we readied our arsenal in accordance with Title 36 CFR Regulations issued previously by the ranger. Pots, spoons, flashlights and golfball-sized rocks were piled neatly at our tent door.

Just as I was lying back, allowing the jagged stones beneath my ensolite mattress to administer acupuncture on my shoulder blades, from the next campsite there came a clatter of pans and frenzied calls of "Hey! A bear!"

"Sounds like they've got the situation under control," I mumbled to Leanne.

"He's after my food!" came a yell.

"Come on, we've got to get up and help," said Leanne, dislocating my knee as she climbed over to unzip the tent. Sadly remembering Title 36 CFR Regulation #4 ("Multiple people chasing a bear greatly increases your effectiveness"), I gathered my weapons and followed.

About 100 yards away we found a solo camper from Santa Cruz. He was thin of limb, with a ponytail and meditation eyes. A highly aggravated bear, 20 feet up in an adjoining tree, growled and snorted in that basically timid way reminiscent of King Kong swatting planes atop the World Trade Center. The bear straddled two limbs, and was busy gnawing on one of them, from which dangled the young man's green food sack.

The bear's strategy was instantly clear to the three members of the park's Dominant Species. He (or maybe it was a she) was going to chew the branch until it fell, and climb down. Then, the furry epicure planned to dine alfresco beneath this very tree or perhaps lumber denward to deliver takeout to the cubs.

Following Title 36 CFR Regulations ("Throw rocks toward the bear. Don't hit other campers.") we let fly a fusillade of granite.

We were three gentle animal lovers, but fear and darkness can do strange things. Instantly, we became fierce hunters; the latest chapter in the long, archetypal conflict of human vs. beast. A thrill of adrenaline surged through me. The bear outweighed all of us together by at least 100 lbs. He could leap down at any moment and sever our neck arteries with one swipe of his catcher's mitt-sized paw. We were unarmed, defending our primitive right to walk through the woods. Anything we could figure out to do seemed fair. I wished I had a few firecrackers. That would scare him away in two seconds flat!

However, high altitude seemed to be exerting some unfortunate and little-known magnetizing effect on the rocks I threw. Not one hit either bear or tree.

But, Thwomp! Someone's rock hit the bear's chest.

Hisssss! replied the bear. He kept on imperturbably gnawing.

The members of the dominant species regrouped. "Ken," said the man, extending his hand, and we introduced ourselves nervously as the branch began to crack overhead.

"Do you think it feels cornered?" wondered Leanne. (The Regulations warned us, "Do not advance on a bear that appears to feel threatened or cornered.")

We decided to back off, let it come down, and then give chase.

"I'd feel a whole lot better if I could grab my food first," said Ken.

Trouble was, he'd have to stand directly under the bear to do it.

"We'll cover you!" cried Leanne, lobbing a stone. I banged and yelled and flashed my light, and Ken leaped forward, severing his food from its rope with one graceful stab of his Swiss army knife.

The hapless bear went right on gnawing until he and the branch came crashing together to the ground. When he discovered his midnight snack was gone, he let forth a sinister growl.

Now was the time to chase. We began hurling more rocks and banging our pots. We didn't want to get too close, though. The bear might notice that the food was now attached to Ken, not the tree, and that Ken was a lot shorter and had fewer limbs.

Title 36 CFR Regulations said to chase the bear, but neglected to say how far. A hundred yards? A quarter mile? The bear was black. So was the night. We settled for chasing him until we lost sight of him, about 20 feet.

Score: Bears, 0; Dominant Species, 1.

Leanne and I returned to our own campsite. Once again, we nestled our vertebrae against the sleeping bag-topped rubble. A minute before, my heart had pounded in fright, but surprisingly, I now became as calm as the San Francisco Financial District on Sunday. I had been skeptical about chasing bears, but I had to admit, being in the Dominant Species felt secure. Before, all I could do was lie awake, staring at the tent's top seam, dreading the sound of claws ripping into the thin nylon walls. Now, Title 36 CFR Regulations permitted me—no, ordered me—to get up and chase bears away. It had been so easy to go mano a mano (well, except for the rocks) with this first bear, and win. I felt groggily heroic. I was even beginning to understand, in a hazy, half-awake way, why hunting and war have been such popular pastimes down through the centuries. I fell into a distilled essence of pure slumber.

In the morning, our red and blue food sacks swayed lazily in the sunlight, just as we had left them the night before. The score was now: bears, 0; humans, 2. I wanted to be jubilant. But daylight was curdling my victory.

It was as if the bear's voice had insinuated itself into my head while I slept. It was saying:

"Look, your species took all the best land. We used to live in San Francisco, and the Central Valley, all up and down the lushest parts of California. There was plenty to eat. Now, you've driven us into these so-called 'wilderness areas' where there's hardly a bug or a berry. You think this paltry diet we get up here is natural for us?

"But when we come down to your towns to dine on your dumpsters, your gardens and your pets, you 'relocate' us right back here. Or worse, you shoot us.

"And then you come up here with salami and Snickers and figs and hurt us with rocks if we try to get them. Come on! Cut us a little slack."

I felt less like a hero and more like a neighborhood bully who had been tormenting a stray dog. On a moral level, the score was: Bears, about 50; Humans, 0. There's got to be a better way for all us creatures to share this gorgeous, granite-strewn spot. Next time a ranger in a bear-proof station instructs me to go into the back country and play the Dominant Species, I may just pass.

MENTAL HEALTH AND THE JOY OF THERAPY

Jennifer Berman

Jennifer Berman

AS SWEET

by Wendy Cope

It's all because we're so alike—
Twin souls, we two.
We smile at the expression, yes,
and know it's true.

I told the shrink. He gave our love
a different name.
But he can call it what he likes—
It's still the same.

I long to see you, hear your voice,
My narcissistic object-choice.

Chris Suddick

CAREER CHANGES

DRILL SERGEANT-TURNED-MALE SENSITIVITY TRAINER

Lori Allen

Mary Lawton

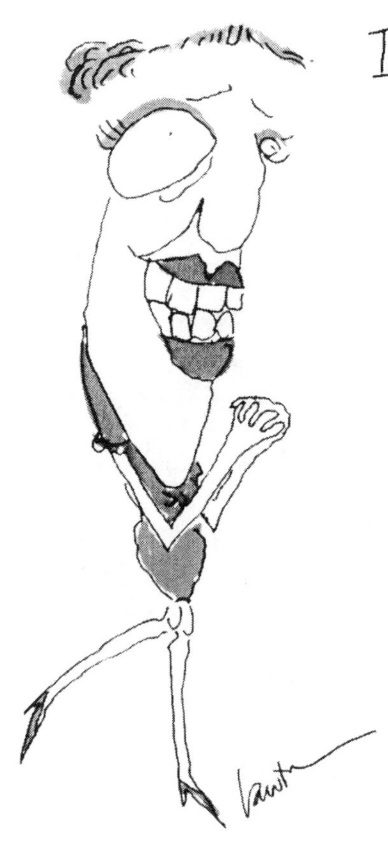

Jan Eliot

NIGHT OF THE LIVING BRA

Suzy Becker

Ellen Forney

Rina Piccolo

Anne Gibbons

Kris Kovick

Jennifer Black Reinhardt

So what exactly does it train them to do?

Kathryn LeMieux

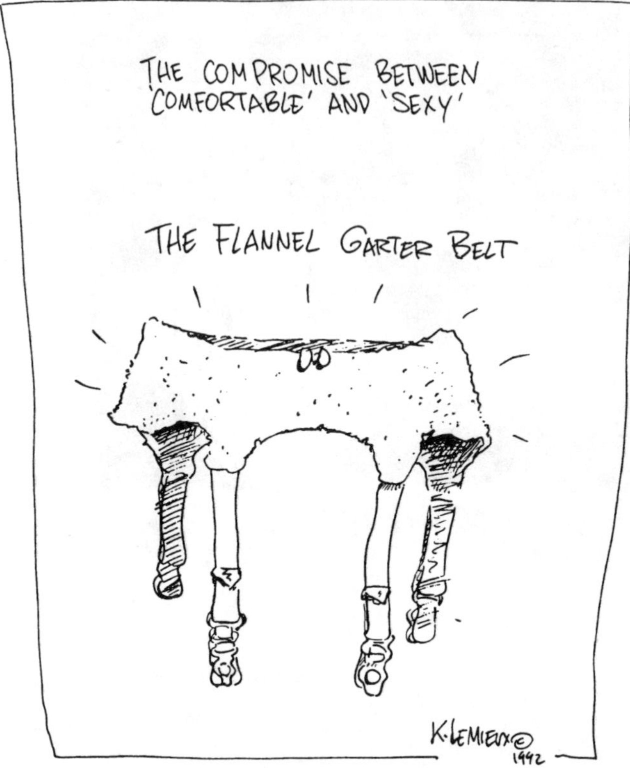

Libby Reid

ARE YOU IN JOB HELL?

So what did you put down for Question 15: 'Have you ever experienced rapture'?

Gail Machlis

Rina Piccolo

Martha Gradisher

RELATIONS WITH CHRIST

by Sibyl James

Stout Mama flips the pages of the job application asking for her work experience, her awards and references, her relations with Jesus Christ. Her relations with Jesus Christ? She knew the university was Christian, but she'd had no idea they'd ask for some pledge of faith, some oath of loyalty to the victims of Roman crucifixions. She considers writing that she watched the hours of Spartacus on TV, despite the constant commercial interruptions, despite the bad dialogue and the silly dimple in Kirk Douglas' chin. Maybe she should say her Catholic family had Christ over every Friday night for fish sticks. Maybe she should tell how breaking up was hard to do. And worth it. She considers lying; she wants this job. She considers taking the high road, explaining that she's nondenominational but full of ethics, that she still supports the Sandinistas, writes checks to Greenpeace and the New El Salvador Today Foundation, that she recycles and sends postcards to Congress protesting against scandals and the cover-up of scandals. She consults a Jewish friend who gives her an answer she knows is theologically confused but semantically perfect in its ambiguity. Under the question about her relations with Christ, she writes "immaculate."

Judy Horacek

INQUIRIES
YOU DON'T HAVE TO BE A SEXIST NEO-FASCIST TO WORK HERE, BUT IT HELPS.
oui?
KAZ ©
YOUR RIGHT TO SMIRK IS RESPECTED. YOUR DECISION NOT TO IS APPRECIATED Management
DUBIOUS CHARITY INVOLVING ANIMALS

REFERENCES

by Flash Rosenberg

Resumes are hilarious to me
precisely because they're SOOOO serious.
I especially howl at the section calling for "references."
Why bother colleagues to write
unread letters about my performance abilities
when there are more direct and reliable options?
Why, I received an excellent recommendation
after my meal in a Chinese restaurant one night:
"You are diligent and hardworking."
A terrific reference!
I taped that fortune to my application.
Besides, it's a great way to test a new employer.
Who wants to work for someone
who doesn't appreciate a recommendation like that?
(I didn't get the job...)

Judy Horacek

HOW DO YOU HATE ME SO FAR?

by Barbara J. Petoskey

"Have a seat, please. It's time for the Company's evaluation of your on-the-job performance."

"Fine, but..."

"Number one, on that outfit you wore your first day: 63% of those surveyed responded, 'Good, but matching shoes would help'; 31% answered, 'Lose the pearls—they went out with Barbara Bush'; and 6% warned, 'Pleats are deadly on a woman your age.' "

"Okay,..."

"Next, regarding your hair style: 45% answered, 'Too light'; 38% said, 'Too long'; 12% asked, 'Have all the beauty salons been closed since 1972'; and 5% looked much worse themselves."

"What the..."

"Then we come to the more serious issue of your name. Let's see, 45% responded, 'What's the matter, isn't her husband's name good enough for her'; a close 43% said, 'Who gives a flying leap'; 9% chose 'Wish I'd thought of that'; and, hmm, a 3% write-in for 'What makes it any of your...' well, moving right along."

"Of course, there's also the matter of your left-handedness. In a modest plurality, 43% believed that a tendency toward the left should not, in itself, disqualify you; 41% agreed, 'It's the efficiency, stupid'; 10% noted, 'There are more of us than you think'; and 6% threatened to protest any purchase of left-handed scissors with company funds."

"But what..."

"More pertinent, certainly, is opinion regarding the selection of your cabinet. Almost three-quarters endorsed your judgment on the expansive, multi-drawer model; 14% expressed reservations that you chose walnut rather than the traditional maple decor; alarmingly, 8% have no idea what you've been doing in your office; and the remainder don't know what they're doing in theirs."

"Lastly, on the matter of expectations: 72% actually like you better than they did at your interview; 21% think it's all downhill from here; and 7% just hope they're still around when you're gone."

"This is all very interesting, but don't you think it's a bit premature? After all, I only started this job last Wednesday."

"Sorry. The honeymoon is over."

Christine Roche

Jackie Urbanovic

BATTLE HYMN OF THE (FEMINIST) REPUBLIC

by Gail White

If the boss is heard to murmur that you have exquisite thighs,
That your bust is 40 inches which is just his favorite size,
And you hesitate to throw a pot of coffee in his eyes,
What can a woman do?

CHORUS
Sue for sexual harassment,
Sue for sexual harassment,
Sue for sexual harassment,
And the cause goes marching on.

If your colleague is promoted just because he has a dick,
If you'd like to grab the boss's neck and give his balls a kick,
If you cannot get a raise because you cannot raise a prick,
What can a woman do?

CHORUS:
Sue for sexual discrimination,
Sue for sexual discrimination,
Sue for sexual discrimination,
And the cause goes marching on.

Anne Gibbons

CONGRATULATIONS!
You're a success!

Judy Horacek

ARE YOU IN JOB HELL?

by Meredith Anthony and Alison Power

1. When you first took your job, you were introduced at a staff meeting by your new boss as:
   a. "My esteemed colleague."
   b. "Tootsie."
   c. "The new babe."
2. The women's lounge where you work is equipped with:
   a. Crabtree & Evelyn soap, a professional makeup consultant and a redwood sauna;
   b. Dispensers of free tampons and condoms;
   c. Fluorescent lights, funhouse mirrors and a calliope.
3. The staff kitchen can produce:
   a. Decaf cappucino with a light dusting of cinnamon;
   b. Mr. Coffee and Little Debbie;
   c. Acute nausea and violent gas.
4. The employee bulletin board is covered with:
   a. Flyers offering free courses for career advancement;
   b. The NBA Playoffs pool;
   c. Clippings concerning homicidal U.S. postal workers with the handwritten comment, "An inspiration to us all!"
5. Your predecessor in the job you hold left you:
   a. A detailed memo, well-organized files and a bouquet of flowers;
   b. Several crises and an assistant who belonged to the Branch Davidians;
   c. A tattered diary that begins, "Call me Ishmael..."
6. Realistically, you can expect a promotion:
   a. In six months to a year, depending on your performance;
   b. When you start wearing short skirts and tight sweaters;
   c. When hell freezes over.

Scoring:

If you answered all or mostly As, you must already be working for yourself or for a family-owned firm run by your mother. Congratulations and please send us the name of the Personnel Director.

If you answered all or mostly Bs, you must work for an authority figure who reminds you of your dad. It may be time for a change.

If you answered all or mostly Cs, you must work in Washington D.C. Get out. Get out now.

MADE YOU LAUGH!

THE CHOSEN FAMILY

by Noreen Stevens

Noreen Stevens

CONTRIBUTORS

Lori Allen, creator of "Nearly Cartoons," is a freelance writer and cartoonist residing in Illinois. Her work has appeared in numerous periodicals and magazines in the Midwest. Ms. Allen is not ashamed to admit she voted for the Clinton/Gore ticket in '92 solely because Al Gore smiled at her once.

Meredith Anthony is one of the authors of *101 Reasons Why We're Doomed* (Avon Books) and a contributing editor to *Hysteria* magazine.

Lynda Barry is a cartoonist and writer whose published works include *The Good Times Are Killing Me* (which was also adapted for the stage), *Down The Street, The Fun House, Big Ideas, Boys and Girls* and *My Perfect Life*. She is a guest commentator on NPR's "All Things Considered" and her illustrations frequently appear in national publications such as *Savvy, Harpers* and *Esquire*. She was a contributor to *Women's Glib* and *Women's Glibber*.

Alison Bechdel has been creating the comic strip "Dykes To Watch Out For" since 1983. Five collections of her work and an annual calendar have been published by Firebrand Books. Her strip is syndicated in over 45 publications in the U.S., Canada and the U.K. Her work has also appeared in *Real Girl, American Splendor, Wimmin's Comix, Gay Comix, Ms., The Village Voice, Women's Glib* and *What Is This Thing Called Sex? Cartoons by Women*.

Suzy Becker is the author of the national best-seller *All I Need To Know I Learned From My Cat* and of *The All Better Book*. She also founded and runs The Widget Factory, a greeting card company in New England, where she lives with her Holstein cat, Binky.

Jennifer Berman lives in Chicago with her two big dogs and one small cat. She runs a postcard company called Humerus Cartoons which features her cartoons on relationships, animals, politics and puns. (You can request a catalog of her postcards by dropping her a line at P.O. Box 6614, Evanston, IL 60624). Carmen Syndication syndicates her weekly cartoons to mostly alternative newsweeklies, but a couple "straight" papers have joined on, like *The San Francisco Chronicle*. Her work has appeared in *Women's Glibber, Kitty Libber* and *Mothers! Ms.* Magazine usually runs her cartoons as well. *Why Dogs Are Better Than Men* (Simon & Schuster/Pocket Books) is Jennifer's first book and you can find it in most bookstores.

Lee Binswanger started drawing single panel comics in 1978 and sold two to *National Lampoon* in 1980. Thirsting for yet more fame, she tried her hand at stories for the underground comics, notably *Wimmin's Comixs*. Her work is in every issue from #8 on. Other publications her stories have been in are *Renegade Romance, Rip Off Comics, Heck!* and *Young Lust*.

Sheree Anne Bradford-Lee is a Canadian writer who has been temporarily imported to Northern California along with her husband. She is currently enjoying the warm weather and other inspiring delights of the area, and doesn't miss the Canadian winters in the slightest. Throughout her recent pregnancy she and her sneer managed quite nicely to stave off the baby patrols.

Barbara Brandon is the only African American female cartoonist currently published in a major U.S. newspaper. Her "Where I'm Coming From" has appeared in the lifestyle pages of *The Detroit Free Press* since June 1989. Universal Press Syndicate is now syndicating her strip nationally. A 1980 graduate of SU's College of Visual and Performing Arts, Brandon has previously worked as a fashion and beauty writer for *Essence* magazine, and as an illustrator for *Essence, The CRISIS*, the *Village Voice* and MCA Records. She resides in New York.

Melinda Brindley is an actress/writer who has written, directed and performed in twelve one-act comedies (under the name Grinding Mills Theatre Company); and has performed in skits she wrote on the cable television show "Sparepartz." Her work has been performed/published elsewhere, including *National Lampoon Magazine*.

Karen Brown: "I made some rather epic sacrifices to become a cartoonist so my attachment to the medium sometimes takes on near-religious proportions. My first exposure to really great, transcendently blow-out cartoons was *RAW*. "City of Love" is my attempt to incorporate some of the weirdness and artfulness of those cartoons in a feature with mainstream (or at least crossover) possibilities. My most grandiose ideal is to do something that raises the standard for cartoon illustration and graphic narratives in broadly distributed publications."

Jessica Bruce's cards can be purchased thru Postscript Cards, Box 61, University Station, Syracuse, NY 13210.

Stephanie Brush: "One thing I want my column to do is provide an outlet for all those people who are a little bit stressed (okay, everyone on Earth) and spare them the trouble of having to go down and deploy nuclear weapons at the supermarket." Stephanie's books include *Life: A Warning* (Simon & Schuster) and *Men: An Owner's Manual*. She graduated from the same high school as Dave Barry, only seven years later.

bulbul cartoons as a feminist, environmentalist and labor advocate. "The world of our species is in its usual state of chaos. I advocate more mental health days off for those in power," she says. After 25 years of cartooning she is still going strong, sending out monthly cartoon packets. Currently a few of her cartoons appear in the *Pete Seeger Songbook, Where Have All the Flowers Gone*.

Jane Caminos is a Brooklyn native, but grew up in New Jersey. She graduated from the Rhode Island School of Design in 1969 and moved to Boston where she began a long, successful career as a designer and illustrator, first in book publishing management and later as an independent. In 1991 she moved her personal life and her business, Illustratus, to Tribeca in New York City. Caminos is also a talented painter who has had numerous one-woman exhibitions of her art. She says that she used to paint "only for relaxation and to combat the rules imposed by commercial work," but in the late 1980s she was convinced by the owner of a gallery in Brookline, MA, to show her work publicly. Since then, her paintings, which *The Boston Globe* called "vivid," have been exhibited in galleries and public spaces throughout Eastern Massachusetts and New York. Caminos says she "came out in the mid-1970s when it was not politically correct to have a sense of humor, and has been waiting all these years for lesbian life to loosen up enough so she could publish" her work.

Martha Campbell is a graduate of Washington University St. Louis School of Fine Arts, and a former writer-designer for Hallmark Cards. A freelance artist since leaving Hallmark in 1968, she has illustrated many books and magazine articles, and around 10,000 of her cartoons have been published in magazines, anthologies and textbooks. A collection of her cartoons was published in 1987. She lives in Harrison, Arkansas, with her husband, two children and cocker spaniel.

Jennifer Camper's cartoons can be found in magazines (*On Our Backs, The Advocate, Out, Hysteria*, etc.), in newspapers (*The Washington Blade, Seattle Twist, Milwaukee In Step, Chicago Nightlines*, etc.), in comic books (*Gay Comics, Real Girl, Dyke's Delight* (U.K.) *Wimmin's Comix*, etc.), in humor anthologies (especially all those fabulous *Women's Glib* collections), on postcards (on sale at your favorite queer bookstore) and on refrigerator doors (Scooter, Fi-fi, Zelda, Big Red, etc.). Her first collection, *Rude Girls and Dangerous Women*, is available from Laugh Lines Press (Box 259/Bala Cynwyd, PA 19004).

Roz Chast's cartoons frequently appear in *The New Yorker, Mother Jones* and *The Sciences*. Her books include *Proof of Life On Earth, The Four Elements, Last Resorts, Unscientific Americans, Parallel Universes, Poems and Songs* and *Mondo Boxo*.

Margie Cherry's cartoon feature "The Art of Motherhood" appears in a Philadelphia-area parenting publication. Her work was featured in *What Is This Thing Called Sex?* and *Mothers!*

Australian cartoonist **Kaz Cooke** is the creator of *The Book of Kazcards: 20 Dead Groovy Tear-Out Postcards For Every Occasion* (Allen & Unwin)

Wendy Cope started writing in 1973. In 1979 her work began to appear in the *Times Literary Supplement* and other periodicals. In 1980 a pamphlet entitled *Across the City* was published by Priapus Press. A selection of her work was included in *Poetry Introduction 5* (Faber 1982). *Making Cocoa For Kingsley Amis* (Faber and Faber), her first collection of poems, was published in 1986 to great critical acclaim—and went straight to the best-seller lists. She is also the author of *Twiddling Your Thumbs*, a book of hand-rhymes for young children, *The River Girl*, a narrative poem, and most recently *Serious Concerns* (Faber), her second collection of poems.

Humor writer and stand-up comic **Cathy Crimmins** is the author of *Curse of the Mommy* and seven other humor books, including the best-selling *Official Yap Handbook*. She's currently working on a humor book about aging baby boomers. She also serves as a creative consultant to many science museums across the country.

Sara Cytron and **Harriet Malinowitz** have been collaborating on Sara's stand-up act for the last six years. *Sojourner* says of them, "It's another Jane Wagner/Lily Tomlin combination—but the *out* version!" Other collaborations include a play, *Minus One*, which Harriet wrote and Sara directed in New York in June 1989. Harriet is currently completing a book on lesbian and gay students in college writing classes, and is also at work on a second play about the lives of two lesbians in their eighties living in Mexico. Sara has performed her lesbian stand-up comedy shows *A Dyke Grows in Brooklyn* and *Take My Domestic Partner—Pleaase!* around the country—in venues ranging from Provincetown to Olivia's 20th Century Anniversary Cruise to Mexico, from the National Women's Studies Association's annual conference to Joan Rivers and Her Funny Friends at New York City's Town Hall. Her work will be featured in *Revolutionary Laughter: The World of Women Comics* (Crossing Press).

Kate DeBold is the political services coordinator at the Gay and Lesbian Victory Fund in Washington D.C. and the author of *Word Gaymes: 101 Puzzles With Lesbian and Gay Themes* (Alyson).

Diane DiMassa is the creator of the gun-toting, grenade-lobbing wonder girl herself: Hothead Paisan, Homicidal Lesbian Terrorist. DiMassa is currently illustrating the *Bible*, and is also working on her autobiography:*Hothead Paisan, Homicidal Lesbian Terrorist*." She lives somewhere near you. (Note: Editor Roz Warren is president of her local chapter of "Hets for Hothead".)

Deb Donnelley works out of her cave in the basement. Other projects include Sisters, a book of photos by her wth text by her playwrite sister, Myra, "Ballroom!" and most recently, "Rocking the Cradle," a collaborative audio-photographic project about women and homelessness. "First Waltz" is from her pin-up calendar, "Brides, Debs and Other Graceful Women We Got to Be."

Andra Douglas: "I graduated with my Bachelors Degree in Communications Design from Florida State University in 1982 and from Pratt Institute with my Master's in Communications Design in 1986. I am currently employed with Time Warner as Creative Director of the video packaging section of Atlantic Records. I created "Sally the Maladjusted" twelve years ago and have had success with her thus far as both a cartoon strip which is published frequently in *Funny Times* and a card line which is being distributed by Recycled Paper Products. Other panel cartoons of mine have been published in magazines such as *Cosmopolitan, Golden Years, Bird Talk* and *Funny Times*."

Debby Earthdaughter. "I'm stressed for survival more than success at this point. I'm 32, white, not able to work due to chronic fatigue and chemical sensitivity."

Jan Eliot is the creator of a weekly 4-panel cartoon strip "Sister City." Her work has appeared in *Women's Glibber, Mothers!* and many other venues. In her spare time, Jan is a full-time advertising designer/copywriter in Eugene, Oregon, and the mother of two grown (brilliant, handsome, strong) daughters. Finding humor in all things has been a necessity for her continued existence. As a young child, she aspired to be Dick Van Dyke (not Rose Marie), and realized the other day that she may have come pretty darn close. Her usual response to life is laughter (and occasional hysteria), and she considers that a great way to be.

Karen Favreau was born and raised in the greater Boston are where she currently lives, scraping by as a struggling cartoonist. Her work appears regularly in *The Valley Comic News* (Northampton, MA), and has appeared nationally in *The Funny Times* and *Factsheet 5*. She plans on attending graduate school in North Carolina next fall so that she can continue to prolong getting a real job.

Nicole Ferentz is an artist/illustrator/greeting card creator/teacher/graphic designer and most recently, letterer, living and working in Chicago. In other words, a Jill-of-all-trades living in a time of postindustrial specialization. She illustrated Celeste West's *Lesbian Love Advisor* (Cleis Press). Her own books include *The 1989 Working Girl's Datebook* (self-published $9.95). *Perky Boo-Boo, Pesky Boo-Boo* (self-published $15.00) and *Recovering From Cancer At Home* (self-published $15.00). Her work was featured in *What Is This Thing Called Sex?*

Cartoonist, screenwriter and former *National Lampoon* magazine editor **Shary Flenniken** lives in Seattle, Washington, and likes to work in her garden, turning over rocks to find the crawly things underneath. Her work was featured in *Women's Glibber* and *What Is This Thing Called Sex?*

Ellen Forney's comics and illustrations have appeared in numerous magazines, newspapers and comic books, including her solo comic book, *Tomato* (to order send 52 cents for a Starhead Comix Catalog to P.O. Box 30044, Seattle, Washington 98103). She lives in Seattle and has no pets, not even a goldfish.

Diane F. Germain is a French-American Feminist-Lesbian psychiatric social worker who recently concluded a strength group for "Women Survivors of Incest and/or Child Molest" which was five years running. She was arrested and jailed for protesting the objectification of women in the "Myth Calipornia Kontest" in 1986. She is a staff cartoonist for *The Lesbian News of Los Angeles*. Her creations have been published in the U.S. as well as England, Canada and Italy. She has created a computer clip art program of diverse women images for Feminists to enhance their desktop publications.

Anne Gibbons seems to be spending a lifetime writing this little bio. She is: happy to be back in New York after living in California for two long years; hoping to publish a cartoon panel called "The Women's Room" in the very near future; working on cartoons, greeting cards and illustrations in her new studio; always wondering where the next idea will come from; often distractable at 41 Union Square, Room 208, New York, NY 10003.

Catherine Goggia has been published in the *1993 Women's Glib Cartoon Calendar, What Is This Thing Called Sex? Cartoons by Women* and her graphics appear on T-shirts and various other surfaces throughout California. Northern Cal readers can catch Catherine's work monthly in *The New Voice*. Catherine is probably working on an illustration right now.

Janis Goodman, vintage 1956, is a freelance cartoonist and illustrator, now living and working in Leeds. She fell into feminism as soon as she heard the word and has seen no reason to run past the "post"! Her work has appeared in *Sour Cream, The New Statesman, Spare Rib, The Guardian, The Yorkshire on Sunday* and many less illustrious titles. She is very grateful to her friends for having interesting lives that she can turn into cartoons, and for being so tolerant of her when she does it (well, mainly!). Her main motto is "Who needs psychotherapy, when you can draw a cartoon about it!"

Hattie Gossett has just finished a book titled *Pussy and Money: Memoirs of a Working Woman*, and another book titled *Cold Sweating and Hot Flashing in the Waiting Room of the 21st Century*.

Martha Gradisher is a freelance cartoonist and comic illustrator living in Nyack, NY, with husband, two boys and dog (a female, just to keep the hormone levels in the house a little more equal).

Roberta Gregory has been doing her best to revolutionize comics for the past 20 years. She was the first lesbian to contribute to *Wimmin's Comix* (1974) and she got kicked out of a lesbian anthology recently for not being lesbian enough. Her current act of subversion is the infamous comic book *Naughty Bits*, available at all really hip comic stores. She's also known for *Artistic Licentiousness, Dynamite Damsels*, and for appearing in practically every issue of *Gay Comics* to date. Send a SASE for her catalog: Roberta Gregory, Box 27438, Seattle, WA 98125.

Jorjet Harper's news, reviews, interviews, and feature articles have appeared in over 30 publications. "A House Is Not A Homo" is reprinted from "Lesbomania," the first collection of her syndicated humor columns (New Victoria Publishers/Box 27/Norwich, VT 05055/ 802-649-5297).

Fate has decreed that **Jane Harty** reside in Brisbane City, Australia, until fame decides to manifest in her life. When not breeding ideas and producing cartoons, Jane tends to her garden of venus fly-traps, wonders what it would be like to be Germaine Greer's brain and is notorious for getting ink all over clothes, important documents and the cat. Her work has appeared in Australian Publications, personal letters to friends and on the occasional dinner napkin.

Dorothy Heller: "My husband and I and our dogs live in the back-of-beyond on a beautiful mountain. I'm a regular contributor to *Midwest Poetry Review*; in addition I'm published in such diverse publications as *Reader's Digest* (who picked up a verse of mine from *The Wall Street Journal*) and a nicely kooky Long Island paper, and (before they stopped printing verse) *The Christian Science Monitor*."

Marion Henley's comic strip "Maxine" is distributed by Carmen Syndicate. Her work has also appeared in many publications whose target audiences run the gamut: Russian feminists, industrial psychologists, "at-risk" teenaged girls, stutterers, recovering scientologists, and (significantly) Hawaiian polygamists.

Nicole Hollander's "Sylvia" strip is syndicated to 46 newspapers. Her books include *Tales From The Planet Sylvia, The Whole Enchilada* and *Everything Here Is Mine: An Unhelpful Guide to Cat Behavior.*

Judy Horacek is an Australian cartoonist and writer based in Melbourne. Her work has been widely published in women's, alternative and community publications, and she produces a range of postcards and greeting cards. *Life On The Edge*, a collection of her cartoons, is available through Spinifex Press, P.O. Box 212, North Melbourne, Vic 3051, Australia (phone Melbourne 329 6088). She also does stand-up poetry and hopes one day to find the perfect way to turn cartoons into a performance art form.

Photographing for thirty years, **Pat Horner** has used her own images as well as appropriated imagery, fabric, string, cellophane, graphite, paint and other materials in these collages, as she moved away from the traditional "pure" photography taught in art and graduate schools. Bringing photography into the fine arts has been her pursuit from the start, which was at a time when much of photography was confined to design or commercial uses. Horner's new work is a sometimes humorous look at society and politics, but behind the humor is a serious description of an unjust situation.

Constance Houck used to be a mime. After a truck hit her head-on she started drawing cartoons. Her work is seen weekly in *XS Magazine* and *The Portland Downtowner.* You can also see her toons in *The Joe Bob Report*. Constance lives in Ft. Lauderdale with Doug, Goat, Lola, Harry and a pink beach cruiser.

Cath Jackson lives and works in London. She has published two collections of her cartoons — *Wonder Wimbin* (Battle Axe Books, 1984) and *Visibly Vera* (Women's Press, 1986). Her work appears regularly in the UK radical feminist magazine *Trouble & Strife,* and has been featured in *Women's Glibber* and *What Is This Thing Called Sex?*

Sibyl James, much like her character Stout Mama, is a leftist feminist who paints her toenails, doesn't shave her legs, and likes to travel. She has taught in the U.S., China, Mexico and Tunisia. "High School Sex" is part of her recent collection of short stories, *The Adventures of Stout Mama* (Papier-Mache Press). James' other books include *In China With Harpo and Karl* (Calyx Books).

Lynn Johnston has won numerous awards, including the Reuben award for Outstanding Cartoonist of the Year (the first and only woman to win this award) from the National Cartoonists Society (NCS) and Best Syndicated Comic Strip (For Better or For Worse) from the NCS. Johnston's home is Ontario, Canada, where she lives with husband Rod and children Aaron and Katie.

Zrinka Jovicic (b. 1967) is a cartoonist living in Zagreb, Croatia. She graduated at the School of Applied Arts in Zagreb. Now she is studying history of art at the University of Zagreb. Her first comics are published in feminist magazine "Kareta." The characters: her boyfriend, sister, parents and friends can easily recognise themselves in the comic situations described in these cartoons (and do not get angry!). For postcards, or other information write: Zrinka Jovicic/ Ljubiciceva 30/4100 Zagreb, Croatia, Europe.

Kris Kovick is currently illustrating the *Bible* from the perspective that it's really a guidebook for the North American Man-Girl Love Association, a how-to book for abusers, perpetrators and child abductors. "I calculate a rape every 2 1/ 2 pages. I am drawing both the old and new testes."

Mina Kumar is an Indian girl in New York. Her work has appeared in *Streetlights* (Viking Penguin), *Christopher Street, Kalliope* and *The Toronto South Asian Review,* among other places. Though wild, she does worry, and does sing the blues.

Joyce La Mers was born in Billings, Montana, but eventually moved to California to experience earthquakes. These and other traumas have provided rich material for her poetry, much of it light verse, which has been appearing for many years in national publications including *The Wall Street Journal, Saturday Evening Post, Light Quarterly, Plains Poetry Journal, The National Enquirer, Verve, Amelia* and others. A former copywriter, she now lives near Ventura, California, where she and her husband run a small manufacturing business.

Adair Lara is an award-winning columnist for the *San Francisco Chronicle* and the author of *Welcome To Earth, Mom!* and *Slowing Down In A Speeded Up World.*

Brenda Lawlor writes a feature column, *Potluck*, which appears in the *Hope Mills Community News* and *Spring Lake News*. Her work has appeared in a variety of publications including *Women's Glibber, Here's To The Land* and *A Time To Listen.* When she's not leading the glamorous life of mother, social worker and writer, she gets in her '87 Subaru and cruises to South of the Border for a free bumper sticker.

Mary Lawton's two cartoon panels, "Nowhere to Hide" and "The Daily Special," appear in newspapers and magazines galore. When she is not drawing or painting she waits on tables at Bette's Diner in Berkeley, which provides the material for many of her cartoons. She also draws "In the Wild," a cartoon strip for young girls in *New Moon Magazine,* and has recently illustrated the *Bette's Diner Pancake Handbook* (Ten Speed Press, 1994).

Carol Lay lives in New York where she produces a weekly cartoon called "Story Minute" that appears in several papers around the country. Two book collections of her work, *Now, Endsville* and *Joyride*, are available through Kitchen Sink Press.

Kathryn LeMieux has done award-winning editorial cartoons for the *Pt. Reyes Light* and the *Marin Independent Journal*. She also did the comic strip "Lyttle Women" for King Features Syndicate. She lives in West Marin County with her husband and son.

Caryn Leschen is a cartoonist and illustrator who has lived in San Francisco for 15 years, but is really from Queens. Her biweekly advice cartoon, "Ask Aunt Violet," appears in a few alternative weekly newspapers (*The SF Weekly; The Ottawa X-Press*) but she'd love to have it in more. If she had more time, she would market herself better, but lately she's been very busy caring for her adorable infant son, Liam. Caryn's work is featured in the *Twisted Sisters* books and in *Wimmin's Comix*, among other venues. She is excited now that she has her very own color TV right on top of her drawing table, and aspires to someday being the only woman on "The Oprah Show" who has never lived in a trailer.

Wendy Lichtman is the author of four books of fiction for children and young adults and has published several personal experience essays in magazines and newspapers. "Needling" originally appeared in *Natural Health Magazine*.

Penny Lorio wears a lot of different hats—as a novelist, playwright and humorist. A lifetime resident of the Great Lake State, she enjoys the simple pleasures of life and making people laugh.

Gail Machlis's single-panel cartoon, "Quality Time," is distributed by Chronicle Features Syndicate. A collection of her work, *Quality Time and Other Quandaries*, was published by Chronicle Books in 1992.

Harriet Malinowitz. See Sara Cytron.

Judy Maclean is a freelance writer and editor whose work has appeared in *The Washington Post, San Francisco Chronicle, In These Times, Sojourner, Funny Times, Out/Look,* and other publications. She is coauthor of *Women Take Care* (Triad Press) and her fiction has been published in *Lesbian Love Stories, Volume II* (Crossing).

Azure Marlowe has hitchhiked through most of the states with her hippie mom. She loves reciting her poetry to whoever will listen. She also likes watching "Good Times" reruns, piercing her ears and meditating to alternative music. In her free time she attends a public high school in Pennsylvania. She hopes some day to graduate from the Peace Corps and work for social justice.

Angela Martin is a well-known cartoonist whose books include *You Worry Me, Tracey, You Really Do!* (The Women's Press) and *A Good Bitch* (The Women's Press). She was a teenage werewolf.

The San Francisco Chronicle called **Sabrina Matthews** "one of the brightest emerging talents in town." Sabrina is an openly gay comic who relates the absurd in everyday life in an uncommon storytelling style. A regular at Josie's Cabaret and Juice Joint and on "the Alex Bennett morning talk show" on KITS-FM, Sabrina has been performing for over two years at gay and lesbian clubs in the Bay Area and has started doing gay material at the Punch Line and other straight clubs, where she has been well received. Having spent most of her adult life traveling and working with children, wood, and tofu, Sabrina became a comic to avoid the last two lesbian professions left open to her: UPS carrier and massage therapist. When she is not trying to find her tiny, hastily scribbled comedy notes in the pile of letters from the IRS on her desk, Sabrina surfs, rides her motorcycle, and plays with her big dog and his cat. All in comfortable shoes. Her work will be featured in *Revolutionary Laughter: The World of Women Comics* (Crossing Press).

Katherine McAlpine is a poet/freelance writer/homesteader/ single parent who lives in Downeast Maine. She bitches on a variety of topics in a variety of literary magazines, and was a recent winner of the "Discovery"/ The Nation Award and the Judith's Room Competition for Emerging Women Poets. Her hobbies include herb growing, beachcombing, wine-making and magic. She will be the Featured Poet in a forthcoming issue of *Light*.

Cinders McLeod developed a sense of justice at the age of five. Since then she has drawn cartoons to expose life's injustices. Her background is Canada, political organising, visual arts, performance, film and music (sings and plays double bass with an album on Billy Braggs Utility Label). She is presently living in Scotland, cartooning for comic books, newspapers, her baby and the world.

Candyce Meherani lives in California where she writes stuff that is certain to be declared great literature as soon as she is dead.

Andrea Natalie was born in 1958, grew up in Arizona and attended Cornell University. In 1980 she moved to New York

The Night Audrey's Vibrator Spoke (Cleis), were both finalists in the Lambda Literary Awards. Her third collection, *Rubyfruit Mountain*, is available from Cleis Press.

Ellen Orleans is a lesbian humorist, speaker and author of *Can't Keep A Straight Face: A Lesbian Looks and Laughs at Life and Who Cares If It's A Choice?* Snappy Answers to 101 Nosy, Intrusive and Highly Personal Questions about Lesbians and Gays (Laugh Lines Press/Box 259/Bala Cynwyd, PA 19004). Her work has appeared in a wide range of publications, from *The Washington Post* to *GirlJock*. When ignoring her deadlines, Ellen can be found fooling around on her Mac or strolling Denver's botanical gardens with her lover, Laurie. Mailing address: Box 1348/Boulder, CO 80306.

Nina Paley, "America's best-loved unknown cartoonist," was born and raised amidst the cornfields of the Midwest. Nina moved to Santa Cruz, California in 1988 with aspirations of becoming a New Age, crystal-wielding hippie. Instead she became a cynical cartoonist. "The pay's not great, but at least I have my integrity, sort of," says the plucky freelance artist from Illinois. Her work has appeared in numerous books and comics including *Grateful Dead Comics, Women's Glibber, Kitty Libber, Choices* and *Dark Horse Presents*. Her weekly comic strip "Nina's Adventures" runs in many newspapers. Two terrific collections of her cartoons are available: *Depression is Fun* (T.H.C. Press) and *Nina's All-Time Greatest Collector's Item Classic Comics #1* (Dark Horse).

Carolyn Parkhurst is a bisexual feminist and a recent graduate of Wesleyan University. Her work has appeared in *Amethyst* and *HotWire*.

Janice Perry is a Vermont-based stand-up comic and cabaret artist whose sharp, funny and political humor is popular with audiences both here and in Europe. Her work will be featured in *Revolutionary Laughter: The World of Women Comics* (Crossing Press).

Paula Peters is a gorgeous, voluptuous, Rubenesque woman who can go from sweetheart to bitch (and back) in 2 seconds flat. She thinks it's a toss-up as to which is better, sex or Snickers. She has been fired from two marriages, and is currently unattached and still searching for a man who is kind and sensitive and whose idea of foreplay is not simply unwrapping a condom.

ous stuff in publications from Maine to Hawaii, includ- *The Women's Glib Cartoon Calendar 1993*. She found refuge in satire during the Reagan-Bush years.

Rina Piccolo's first cartoon collection, *Stand Back, I Think I'm Gonna Laugh*, was recently published (to great critical acclaim) by Laugh Lines Press (Box 259/Bala Cynwyd, PA 19004). Her work has appeared in *The Utne Reader, Funny Times, Comic Relief, Women's Glibber, Kitty Libber,* and *What Is This Thing Called Sex? Cartoons by Women*. She is forever making up funny stuff and would like to hear from anyone who cares. Write: R. Piccolo/1026 Dovercourt Road, Toronto, Ontario, CANADA M6H 2X8.

Stephanie Piro's first cartoon collection, *Men! Ha!*, was recently published (to great critical acclaim) by Laugh Lines Press (Box 259/Bala Cynwyd, PA 19004). Her designs appear on coffee mugs, T-shirts, bottons and more. For a catalog write: Box 605/Farmington, New Hampshire 03835.

Alison Power is a coauthor of *101 Reasons Why We're Doomed* (Avon Books).

Viv Quillin. Born 1946 (they stopped the war specially). Raised in the Derbyshire countryside. Married. Discovered sense of humor when three kids arrived in quick succession. Divorced. (He kept the house and cash and she kept the three gorgeous kids.) Became cartoonist. Over past dozen years has written and cartooned five of her own books and illustrated lots of other people's work. Appeared in *Women's Glibber, What Is This Thing Called Sex?, Cosmopolitan, Family Circle, Spare Rib, Everywoman, New Internationalist, Evening Standard* and *Cath Tate Cards*. Her work has been translated into many different languages. Currently lives in Oxford and working on a cartoon book of cats, the content of which is at present a deep secret.

Libby Reid grew up in West Virginia and the suburbs of Washington, D.C. She worked as a waitress, cheese hostess, glamorous fashion model, radio announcer and graphic art slave before finding her true calling as a cartoonist. Her first book was *Do You Hate Your Hips More Than Nuclear War?* Next came *You Don't Have To Pet To Be Popular*. She now dwells in New York City where she likes to notice stuff.

Jennifer Black Reinhardt is the illustrator and, usually, author of a line of greeting cards called Rhinestones for

Renaissance Greeting Card Co., Springvale, ME. She also illustrates two hilarious calendars called *Cat Codependence* and *Dog Codependency* (for people who love their cats/dogs *too* much). She's currently working on a children's book and lives in Pennsylvania with her beloved husband, Joe, and cat/child Maxfield. She also thinks it's really silly to be talking about herself in the third person.

Dianne Reum: "I can eat more chocolate without throwing up at one sitting than anyone I know but since you can't make a career out of that, I cartoon. (I haven't made a career out of cartooning, either, but at least cartooning doesn't give me zits.) (I do, however, throw up from time to time.) I've been published in *Playgirl, Ms.*, and many anthologies (including these fun books, all edited by the ever-positive Roz Warren: *Women's Glibber, Mothers!, What is This Thing Called Sex?, Kitty Libber* and *Weenie-toons.*

May Richstone. "My bio (published in *Light* and *Wall Street Journal*):

Harvest
I sowed wild oats
In my green age
And now in autumn
I grow sage."

Trina Robbins has been drawing comics for publication for so many years that she no longer remembers the names of all the comics she's done. Her latest book, however, is called *A Century Of Cartoonists.* She has entirely too many cats and would rather be in Hawaii.

Flash Rosenberg "In a persistent, but vain, attempt to understand life (or merely to amuse friends and seduce lovers) I blurt ideas in spoken, written, sketched, sewn, photographed and filmed forms. My cartoons air as the radio spots 'Flash Moments,' weekday mornings on the public radio station WXPN-FM in Philadelphia. 'Flashpoint cartoons' have appeared in *The New York Daily News, The Village Voice, The Philadelphia Inquirer, The Funny Times,* and *Hysteria*. I've taught college, got grants, lived in France, made films, had gallery exhibitions, worked in a museum, lifeguarded, misjudged, was a photographer, won prizes, had my heart broken and raised turtles. Instead of jobs, I have schemes. My favoite color is 'clear.' My favorite answer is 'okay.' I am bi-Ziptual, occupying both 19107 and 10018 to do my work." Her work will be featured in *Revolutionary Laughter: The World of Women Comics* (Crossing Press).

Sharon Rudahl. "Born 1947, Arlington, Virginia. BFA Cooper Union 1969. Beatnik, hippie, Luddite. Painter, poet, pornographer, photographer, history teacher, tournament chess player, technical illustrator—but most often gainfully employed. Professional chess player husband, two highly gifted sons and one very fat Siamese cat."

Rita Rudner is a popular stand-up comic and comic actress and the author of *Naked Beneath My Clothes* and *Ruta Rudner's Guide To Men*. Her work will be featured in *Revolutionary Laughter: The World of Women Comics* (Crossing Press).

Betsy Salkind is a comedian/performance artist/writer. Her early comedy years were spent in Boston with such groups as Guilty Children, Terrorist Bridesmaids (4 comediennes determined to get a second use out of those dresses) and The Other White Meat. She is known for her intelligent, dark humor and such characters as "Squirrel Lady" and "The Godmother," and her impersonation of Margaret Thatcher. She was in the cast of WGBH's "The World According to Us," and recently shot her first feature film, *Lost Eden,* in which she played Girl #1. She currently resides in NYC, with her cats Rotunda and Boutros Boutros-Ghali. Her work will be featured in *Revolutionary Laughter: The World of Women Comics* (Crossing Press).

Liz Scott is the author of *Never Heave Your Bosom In A Front Hook Bra* and *Never Sleep With A Fat Man In July.* She lives in New Orleans with her husband and six children.

Amy Sibiga is a photographer/graphic designer who finds it a great pleasure to be included in one of Roz's humor collections.

Probably one of the millions of women fooled into thinking that a mother can very easily work from home while raising a baby, the now much wiser **Theresa Henry Smith** is presently getting a reality check. Learning new computer programs while braving milk blisters from breastfeeding is no picnic! Theresa hopes the experience might someday be expressed in the way of a cartoon book or comic. Correspondence with other moms who'd like to share their humourous experiences or anecdotes are most welcome! If you aren't too harried please write: Theresa Henry Smith, 201 Clinton Place, New Westminster, B.C., Canada V3L-1J1.

Lori Sprecker is the author of *Anxiety Attack* (Violet Ink) and *Sister Safety Pin* (Firebrand).

Noreen Stevens is a comic and activist living in Winnipeg, Manitoba, Canada.Her cartoon strip "The Chosen Family" appears in periodicals and anthologies throughout North America. As well, she is one half (with photographer Sheila Spence) of Average Good Looks, a terrorist girl-gang of two, which creates queer positive billboard and text images for display anywhere and everywhere. Assorted work appears in *Women's Glib* and *Weenie-toons*. Noreen illustrated Ellen Orlean's *Can't Keep A Straight Face* (Laugh Lines Press).

Chris Suddick is a freelance cartoonist and happily married mother of none. Her comic strips "OFF101" and "Valley Alley" have been published by *The San Jose Mercury News* since 1989.

Bonnie Timmons is a popular Pennsylvania-based cartoonist and the author of *Anxiety* (Fawcett Columbine).

Jackie Urbanovic has been working as a cartoonist/illustrator for the past 15 years though she is relatively new to the comics industry. Her cartoons can be found in *Wimmin's Comix, Strip AIDS U.S.A., Choices, In Stitches, Images of Omaha, Women's Glibber* and *The 1993 Women's Glib Cartoon Calendar*.

Nicole S. Urdang, a writer and psychotherapist in private practice, has had essays, short stories and poems published in *Libido, Words on Paper, Psychopoetica* (U.K.), *Common Ground, The Buffalo News, Radiance*, and others. Recently, she has been working on a series of short stories whose unifying theme is "Different Realities." She is married and has two children.

Robin Watkins. "Don't worry, mom. I'm studying something sensible when I go back to school this fall. Were you ever worried, Jim Davis?"

Gail White edits poetry for the *Piedmont Literary Review* from her English cottage in Breaux Bridge, LA. Her own poetry will appear in the *Boxcars Anthology* from Summer Stream Press in 1994. She has been called "America's neglected major poet" by such eminent critics as her husband and parents.

Born in the depths of the baby boom, **Signe Wilkinson** graduated from her suburban Philadelphia high school the year the SAT scores began their slide. After acquiring a B.A. in English from a western university of middling academic reputation, Wilkinson was pathetically unprepared for real work...so became a reporter, stringing for the *West Chester* (PA) *Daily Local News*. Wilkinson began drawing about the people she was supposed to be reporting on. She realized cartooning combined her interests in art and politics without taxing her interest in spelling. She began freelancing at several Philadelphia and New York publications, finally landing a full-time job at *The San Jose Mercury News* in 1982. Her 3 1/2 years there were stormy but deeply instructive. Wilkinson repaid her long-suffering Mercury News editor by taking a job at the *Philadelphia Daily News*, where she has been drawing contentedly ever since. Wilkinson values her intensely unremarkable family life, she gardens, and every Monday night she irons her beloved husband's shirts while watching "Murphy Brown."

ABOUT THE EDITOR

Roz Warren is the editor of the ground-breaking Women's Glib humor collection. She is a happily married radical feminist mom, grew up in Detroit, graduated from The University of Chicago and received her law degree from Boston University Law School. Roz practiced law until the birth of her son, six years ago. Now an at-home mom, she spends Quantity Time with son Thomas.

OTHER HUMOR BOOKS BY ROZ WARREN

Women's Glib: A Collection of Women's Humor
Women's Glibber: State-of-the-Art Women's Humor
Glibquips: Funny Words by Funny Women
What is This Thing Called Sex?: Cartoons by Women
Kitty Libber: Cat Cartoons by Women
Mothers!: Cartoons by Women